Salamander Dreaming

The story of George
and Jean Russell

as told to
Steve J Plummer

Salamander Dreaming

First published 2006

First published 2006 by
Exposure Publishing,
an imprint of Diggory Press
Three Rivers, Minions, Liskeard, PL14 5LE
WWW.DIGGORYPRESS.COM

ISBN 1-84685-222-6
978-1-84685-222-0

Copyright ©
Steve Plummer, Jean Russell, George Russell
2006

Conditions of sale
This book is sold subject to the conditions that it shall not, by way of trade or otherwise, be lent, re-sold, hired out or otherwise circulated without the prior permission of the copyright holders. No part of this publication may be reproduced, stored in a retrieval system or transmitted in any form or by any means without the prior permission of the copyright holders.

Cover design
From photographs by Jean Russell

Cloth Wrap Publishing
2006

For

Kim, Tania, Zoe and Chris

FOREWORD

I first met Jean and George Russell in early 2001. They were sitting, comfortably reclined, on a pair of travel worn deckchairs. They were each gazing happily at nothing in particular, enjoying the Mediterranean sun.

George tickled the ear of his large, somnolent dog, Scrumpy, while Jean absently turned the pages of a yellowing paperback.

They were seated in the middle of a gravel road, apparently impervious to the possibility of stray traffic interrupting their day. The chances were slim; they were seated outside their timber chalet on a campsite a few kilometres west of the picturesque holiday town of Nerja on the Costa del Sol.

While Nerja had been known to entertain a traffic jam or two, this upper reach of Camping el Pino seldom saw more than the electric scooter George had bought his granddaughter to mark her fourteenth birthday.

At first glance Jean and George seemed to be, as indeed they were, a pleasantly relaxed yet unconventional retired couple, bringing up their granddaughter in the slow paced warmth of southern Spain.

Scratching ever so tentatively through their genial surface was to reveal a generosity that is now all but extinct.

This, perhaps, is as it should be. In many ways Jean and George are the products of a different era. They yearn for a time when a favour performed for a neighbour – or a total stranger – was a daily event. They have remained unmoved by changes in technology or social attitude and by those they stumble across who fail to share their view of life.

Jean, full of homespun wisdom, the model for any would-be favourite aunt, is as open, honest and trusting as George is quiet and thoughtful.

Seeing my approach, George rises slowly from his seat, extending a shovel hand in welcome.

At his gentle request, Jean withdraws to their porch, pulling a bicycle to one side to reveal a battered fridge. Returning with a few bottles of cold beer, George towers over her like a great benevolent bear. As one hand envelopes a bottle, the other gently strokes her back until she resumes her seat again.

As we settle down for another chat, I am reminded that the small space they call home had, for many years, been portable and temporary. Once again, it is surrounded by battered suitcases, cardboard boxes and bags, all waiting to be either filled or moved to their next home.

They have moved twice in the last 12 months and are about to move again. They have been in their present home for six months and are half way through packing. Within the next six months they would travel 3,000 miles round northern France in search of yet another new address.

Jean and George have always enjoyed peace and quiet. As George takes a sip from his beer, he nods in the direction of their nearest neighbour; a pair of large tents pitched some thirty feet up the avocado covered slope. The Spanish occupants have rented their pitch for a year. Every weekend two families appear and set up a large barbeque. The trouble was, George laments, they just won't stop *talking*.

It was enough to drive Jean and George away; a process they were so well practiced at, they needed no plan or rehearsal. Their worldly goods would quickly be transferred from chalet to their ancient Winnebago camper van, and be spirited away to pastures new.

On this occasion, however, their move would take them no further than the other side of the site to another timber chalet. Had so convenient an alternative not become available, we might never have become embroiled on the subject of George's long time love of the sea.

When Jean dropped into one of our conversations that they had once been shipwrecked, I remember feeling absolutely no sense of doubt or surprise whatever.

I became quickly magnetised to their relaxed revelations and when Jean mentioned she had also kept a diary, I was immediately hooked.

What follows is Jean and George's story. It is dedicated to all those brave enough, (or foolhardy enough, depending on your point of view) to drop all they have worked for in search of escape. It is especially for their children Kim and Tania, their friend Zoe and for Chris, sadly missed, who loved the all too brief time she enjoyed in their company on Camping el Pino.

INTRODUCTION

Not everyone who is shipwrecked lives the life of Robinson Crusoe.

There are those whose ships are wrecked in lands far from the uninhabited desert island of Daniel Defoe's southern ocean.

For some castaways, finding shelter and producing fire are the least of their problems.

Their greatest threat comes not from those assumed to be cannibals by more 'civilized' folk and called savages. All too often it stems from the very people we have given the power to help us. Such authority carries with it responsibility, especially at moments of crisis. While we are urged to put our trust in them, they don't always rise to the challenge and their victims are the very people they are supposed to serve.

But every castaway should have a Man Friday.

CHAPTER ONE

Beginnings

It all started over the Christmas holiday of 1978.

An old pal of George's had just returned from a prolonged holiday and was now back in our native island of Guernsey. Eager to renew old friendships, since his return he had entertained us with unending tales of his life both before and since his decision to sell up and move to the Bahamas.

That had been 15 years earlier and since then he had, at least by his own account, made an excellent living, thoroughly enjoying himself along the way.

His exploits never failed to get our imaginative juices going. Possibly helped by a niggling fear that we were slipping into a rut, these reminiscences gave us thoroughly itchy feet. They also fanned our desire to explore well beyond the sandy beaches of our comfortable little island.

When George and I thought about it – and we often did – we couldn't even remember the last time we had ventured far enough, or for long enough, to claim we had been on holiday.

We had been too busy bringing up our two daughters, Kim and Tania, aged five and four. Every drop of spare cash was used either on them or renovating the old cottage we now lived in, inherited from George's parents.

These happy discussions became our 'If' evenings. There is a lot of fun in the word 'if'. It lends freedom to the imagination. The walls fall away and the horizon seems an altogether more exciting place. The more 'ifs' there were, the more barriers that had previously seemed impenetrable dissolved before the eyes.

"If we could just take a holiday abroad ..."

"If we could just travel the world ..."

"If we could just sell up everything and go ..."

It was at about this time that we met and became friendly with our not too distant neighbours, Colin and Barbara. We took an immediate liking to them and visited each other regularly. Each successive visit saw us convincing ourselves – and each other – that our 'ifs' could become a reality.

Opportunity was, we told ourselves, staring us in the

face... We owed it to ourselves... It would be a wonderful education for the children... There was nothing to keep us on the island... There was nothing to hold us back.

We had convinced ourselves. Our 'if' became 'when'. The blank, glazed looks with watery eyes focused somewhere in the middle distance became focussed and sharpened. Daydreaming was replaced by planning, accountancy, timetables and lists of thing to do.

Almost without realising it, a decision was made. Looking back now, I don't think any of us really know who made it or exactly when it happened.

One morning, similar to any other, I woke just in time to see George's large frame retreating down our stairs. It was a sunny day and I climbed out of bed, opened the bedroom window and waved him off to work. And there it was, staring back at me as if challenging me to change my mind; a large sign in the front garden with the words 'for sale' printed boldly across it. George paused beneath it, his thumbs resting in his leather belt as he gazed up at the words. He turned back to me at my window, stuck his thumb up in the air and strolled through the gate.

My poor family paid an immediate toll. Each time a car rolled towards us down our narrow lane, cushions were shaken and plumped up, ashtrays hastily emptied and toys scurried out of sight under the settee or into a cupboard.

Every time a car slowed or its occupants so much as glanced at our 'for sale' sign I convinced myself, watching from the front window, this was a 'P.P'. A Prospective Purchaser.

Anyone who has ever tried to sell a property, especially when it is to fulfil a dream, will recognise the symptoms; the aerosol of air freshener forever within easy reach. The sweaty palms. The panic that directions given by the estate agent (who of course you never entirely trust) weren't sufficient to guide the buyer to your front door. The fear that the asking price is too high, or worse – too low.

Should we have redecorated the spare bedroom ? Had I remembered to make the girls' beds ? Is it too pushy to offer the next P.P a cup of coffee ? Should there be biscuits ? Are we right to follow the advice of our well meaning neighbour and allow the smell of percolating coffee to waft temptingly through the house ? I made a mental note: must buy a coffee percolator.

And should we have moved the sideboard to cover that embarrassing mark on the living room wall?

Our plan was, on the face of it, simplicity itself. We would sell the house, place all our furniture in the hands of a local auctioneer and dispose of our small rust ridden car for the best price we could get.

The proceeds from all of these would be used to purchase a suitable boat in which to travel the seven seas. Thereafter, good times and a comfortable living were sure to follow.

An early problem was our respective definitions of the word 'suitable'. George thought of it as meaning a working vessel that we could use in and around the Mediterranean for charter, salvage or diving. His 'suitable' also included a minimum specification relating to tonnage, beam, and engine size.

I knew little of these things. For my part, the important element in the plan was where the said boat was going to take us. I cared little how heavy, long or fat it was or the trade it was put to when it got there. The crucial factors were that there would be a deep blue sky, constant sun and acres of hot white sand on which to tan my bronzed body (when it became too lazy to swim in the clear sea between coral and brightly coloured fish). Provided there was enough space on the deck to stretch out on, I cared not a jot what sort of work it was capable of.

I kept my thoughts and dreams to myself. George and Colin were clearly not receptive enough yet. Their conversations consisted of nothing more important than boy's talk. Sail versus engine. Diesel or petrol? Generators, pumps, pulleys and anchors; the number and weight to be carefully calculated against tonnage and payload. Radio and radar, navigation and admiralty charts, compasses and chronometers – whatever all that meant. I understood none of it, so it was obviously irrelevant to our overall strategy.

George had some experience with boats, having spent three years as a ship's engineer aboard an 80 ft. salvage schooner. He had also had some lessons in navigation from a friend who had been the captain of an Esso tanker. (The ones that dominates the shipping lanes, not the lanes between petrol stations).

Our friend Colin had spent some time crewing yachts

around the Mediterranean. He was also a mechanic, heavily built and stood 6ft 4in. in his bare feet. As George had concluded, he was a handy bloke to have around in an emergency. Not that we intended to have any of those, of course.

Just as importantly, his wife Barbara was a nurse. While we also knew we would never need her services either, it would be reassuring to have her around.

I had surprised myself at just how uncharacteristically sensible and practical we seemed to be becoming. Whether or not we were just trying to reassure ourselves, we found we were regularly congratulating each other on the value of our collective skills and experience.

We knew we would need a crew of at least five, and preferably six. Of all our other friends, John and Paula had, at first, been amongst the very few who hadn't dismissed our early dreams out of hand. They had been swept along by our tide of enthusiasm and had even engaged themselves in our planning sessions. They were clearly willing (and very able) and when they started dropping hints about coming with us we had no hesitation in inviting them.

They were true islanders. Never out of a pure white T-shirt in summer or winter, John was the proud owner of a stout little timber yacht. Both he and Paula had been brought up in and around St.Peter's Port. They were often seen skitting across the harbour between the wealthy visitors' booze cruisers and recently had begun moaning even more volubly than most about the increasing tide of seasonal visitors. John's latest T-shirt bore the motto *'I'm not a tourist. I bl**dy live here !'*. More importantly, both he and Paula knew the tides and currents between the islands and the northwest tip of France better than most people knew their route to work.

All in all, I felt we were in safe hands and were happy to let the lads have their nautical discussions while I discussed the more important things – like food, clothes and soap – with Barbara and Paula. We met each Sunday evening to discuss our latest ideas and refine the grand plan.

Meanwhile, our other friends continued to humour us. Whenever mention was made of 'our boat' (which we hadn't even found yet, but that didn't seem to matter) they would sigh and nod understandingly.

These 'landlubbing' friends and neighbours – those who were to be left behind – split themselves into two camps. There were the sighers and nodders; those who simply didn't believe anything would come of it. Then there were the friends who laughed and humoured us until, huddled together round the tables of the Ship and Anchor, privately declared their conviction that we were completely mad.

We didn't know it at the time, but when the landlord suggested that one day soon the 'for sale' board would be pulled down, they opened a book.

Odds were carefully worked out and bets placed on the date one of us would admit the idea had been shelved. Good money was put on the cottage never being sold, on our failing to buy a boat and our never leaving port.

Judging by the odds, they were universally sure we would soon 'come to our senses' and everything would get back to normal. (Whatever 'normal' is).

There were others, well meaning and sincere, who set out to actively discourage. We should think, they urged, of the security we would be throwing away. The comfortable life on our lovely island and cosy little Carey Cottage, all thrown up – for what ? We should appreciate what we had, they told us. Many would sell their souls for the life we have.

What we had was a happy rut. And we were determined to climb out of it.

Unmoved by sceptics or common sense, and in anticipation of a successful house sale, we had been buying yachting magazines. George, Colin and John spent much of our Sunday evenings swotting over these and various other seafaring publications.

The more they read, the more enthusiastic they became, infecting us with expectation and images of Atlantic cruisers.

It was some five weeks after the idea had been hatched that George suddenly stopped reading. His index finger plunged onto the open page before him.

"That's it." The rest of us looked at him expectantly. "'*The Deep Diver*'. She's 97 ft. with a 23 ft. beam. 240 horse power Crossley engine. That's the one."

We looked around the table, testing each other's reactions. It was Colin who finally broke the silence.

"How much ?"

George's head dropped to the page again, running his finger along the print, for all the world as if he hadn't already seen, noted and made mental calculations of the cost. "£26,000."

There was another pause. George looked up as if surprised to the point of being hurt at the lack of response. "Well it's got to be worth a look hasn't it ?"

We all nodded, murmuring collective agreement. There was, however, one little detail which George hadn't immediately volunteered. The Deep Diver was berthed in Belfast.

George was elected to make a 'phone call and obtain more details. He licked the end of a stub of pencil, waiting for the reply. The rest of us sat in silence, staring at him.

"Yes, hello." We all jumped. George's voice always rose a few decibels when he was on the 'phone. We edged forward, as if by doing so we might be able to hear the voice at the other end of the line.

"Your advert... Deep Diver. Yes... 97 ft., 23 ft. beam... Yes ? When was she built ? ... Really ? ... Right... Really ? And what capacity...I see... Really ?"

I tried to read George's face. I have always been able to tell a certain amount of what he is thinking by just looking. He turned away slightly, burying his chin into his breast bone and scribbling on the back of an envelope.

"Uh-ha. Yes. Yes ... Really ?"

I looked surreptitiously over his shoulder. His large hand moved to a better position to write, almost inadvertently resting across the paper and blocking my view. He nodded down the 'phone as his pencil jerked and scraped.

"And what sort of... Uh-ha. Yes. I see."

Eventually, he replaced the receiver and sat back, lifting his scrap of paper and silently reading what he had just written. He inhaled deeply.

Colin broke the tension. "Well ? Are you going to tell us ?"

George nodded once. "Deep Diver", he announced, "was built in 1945 as a supply ship for the Admiralty." He smiled slightly. "That's a good sign. The Navy wouldn't commission a vessel that hadn't been properly built."

Her career had, since then, taken several strange turns. She had been used during the 1960's as the base for Radio

Caroline. She had moored in the North Sea, just outside Britain's territorial waters and perilously close to the main shipping lanes. Another good sign, George concluded.

"If she can stay afloat in the North Sea, she'll eat up the Mediterranean." He smiled encouragingly at our gathered faces. John glanced at Colin, the slightest hint of doubt flickering between them.

My memory went back to the fuzzy and sometimes incoherent cracklings of my old transistor radio. How often I had been told by my friends of a (very slightly !) younger generation how, as children, they used to crouch under their bedclothes at night, listening through a plastic earpiece, illicitly trying to tune in to 208 metres on the medium wave. Being deafened by piercing whistles, crackles and hissing all became worthwhile when occasionally rewarded by the excitement of Radio Caroline filtering through the ether. Radio Luxembourg might have been regarded by some as more trendy but, for the majority, reception was so poor as to render the whole process quite pointless.

After a spell being used as a diving and salvage vessel, for which she had been given her present name, Deep Diver had for the last 18 months been used again as a pirate radio ship, this time dodging Spanish, French and Italian authorities by sailing up and down the Mediterranean.

There was something perversely appealing about an Admiralty vessel being used to break the law (particularly a law as seemingly pointless as one which limits broadcasting) which drew George and Colin to take a week off work to go and look her over.

When they got back to Guernsey a week later, they were full of enthusiasm for The Deep Diver. She was indeed a working vessel – not the three mast schooner or barque I had secretly (and perhaps romantically) been hoping for. But, they enthused, she had a huge winch ! This seemed to make up for virtually any possible deficiency, so far as they were concerned. Not that they mentioned any deficiencies.

Every so often over the days that followed, George and Colin were heard to exchange remarks such as "That compressor will be a boon", and "the anchor's a real cracker."

More, I suspected, for their wives' benefit than for their own, nothing could compensate for the lack of Onedin Line style clipper. I still dreamed of running before the wind, sails full, her master's nut brown features shaded from the sun by his white beard and weathered cap...

The Deep Diver, so far as George and Colin were concerned and from their glowing description, was the perfect vessel. Despite my silent dreams, George and Colin were getting down to details now. She had ten births and a huge forward hold. Even if she didn't have the sails we had hoped for, she did have two massive steel radio masts!

Gradually I was won round. We had visions of doing salvage work and of taking parties of recreational divers out to explore reefs, lagoons and wreck sites. We could transport local cargoes in the off season or if more exotic work didn't come our way. The possibilities seemed endless for an enthusiastic crew with a good sound working vessel.

George, it turned out, had also been formulating plans to convert her to sail. If we could raise the necessary cash – and find timber masts to suit – we would eventually save a fortune on fuel. I nodded eagerly, seeing at least one part of my dream becoming a possibility again.

"Tourists", I reminded him, "will love that. They'll be much more willing to pay for trips under sail." I smiled up at him, resting my hand on his heavy forearm. "You're brilliant, George. Just brilliant."

By the end of that first week after their visit to The Deep Diver, we were all exhausted by the increasing list of projects and tasks we would put her to. There was, however, one small thing that Barbara and I should be aware of.

She was, they warned, just a bit dirty.

Barbara shrugged and we nodded to each other. "We've got kids." I told her. "We can cope with a bit of dirt."

Our next priority was to sell the cottage. Well, let's be honest, our next priority was to find a buyer, then negotiate a price, instruct a solicitor, haggle over fixtures and fittings ... If you've been through the mill of buying or selling a house, you'll know what I mean!

We were asking for the seemingly vast sum of £25,000 and were quite encouraged by the number of 'P.P's' we had seen. We had never lived so tidily and the aroma of coffee had never been so powerful. Our little home had never seen so many visitors.

The owner of the Deep Diver in Belfast was a Mr Hughes, and he was becoming impatient. Were we going to cough up the cash, he wanted to know. We had to understand, he had other people interested. People who were offering to pay immediately. Could we at least pay a deposit?

We mumbled our excuses, begged for a little more time. Just as all seemed likely to be lost and minutes after Mr Hughes had told us for the third time about a Scottish fisherman wishing to extend his fleet, one of our P.P's made an offer.

We decided to put our cards on the table. We invited the purchaser to call and see us to discuss the details.

We told him, bluntly, that we needed a deposit, post-haste. He agreed there should be no problem, but was curious to know why we were in such a hurry.

I glanced at George. He gave wordless assent. The man deserved an explanation.

"We're buying a boat." I told him. "We've got to complete the sale quickly on the cottage or we'll lose it."

The buyer smiled and nodded. We had no reason to worry. He didn't need a mortgage and assured us we could safely go ahead and pay our deposit on The Deep Diver. He would arrange to transfer his deposit to our bank the next morning.

A quick visit to the local bank manager and a combination of self confidence and pleading, combined with a bit of arm twisting persuaded him, reluctantly, to provide a £17,000 bridging loan. There was just one condition; the bank must receive our house buyer's deposit by the end of the week.

George rose from his chair, eager to conclude the discussion.

"That's not a problem." He shook the bemused bank manager by the hand. "The chap buying the house said he's send the deposit today."

Everything seemed, at last, to be moving. George and Colin took another week of their annual holiday and prepared to travel back to Belfast.

It was, of course, too good to last. Within days, fate, boat seller and house buyer conspired to thoroughly gum up our plans.

In order to bring the price of the boat down from £26,000 to £20,000 they had negotiated that various items be removed prior to our taking delivery of her.

Belfast at this time was going through an even rougher period than usual. Although we were largely sheltered from any repercussions in the Channel Islands, we couldn't avoid the mayhem on the TV news and in the newspapers.

Various renegade bands of Republicans and Loyalists seemed intent on inflicting as much damage as they could on each other and any other opponents of their respective causes. The politicians and armed forces seemed powerless to stop the troubles and a week seldom went by without news of a shooting or bomb explosion either in Ireland or England.

When our would-be boat buyers arrived in Belfast and were asked by the security officer on duty the nature of their business in the Province, their straight forward answers met with more than a little suspicion. The officer drew in his breath and removed his cap to scratch a balding scalp; an action he was to repeat several times before their conversation was over.

"So, you've come to Northern Ireland to buy a boat ?"

They nodded and picked up their bags to leave. It seemed, to them, a perfectly satisfactory conclusion to a routine enquiry.

"Are there not enough boats in the Channel Islands ?"

There was something in the officer's tone which made George and Colin put their bags down again.

They explained how they had this vision ... this dream ... they were not after just any boat - at least, not the sort you could see in abundance in St.Peter's Port, Havelet Bay or any one of half a dozen other fashionably expensive mooring places around the islands.

Noting the officer's apparent confusion, George tried to explain.

"Those are flashy yachts built for people with money, not for sailing people." The officer seemed not to understand the nautical disadvantages of recreational vehicles. "They're for weekend sailors who just skip between the islands. They probably have a crew to do the sailing for them, anyway."

George and Colin snorted to each other, mutually understanding the hopeless condition of the leisure sailor. The security officer still failed to grasp the significance. "Well, they might get as far as the north coast of France or up to Southampton or Weymouth occasionally, but that's all." George tapped his open palm with a solid index finger. "What we want is a good, strong working vessel. The boat we're after must be capable of far more than... than *booze cruising*. And stowage. She must have a large hold." Colin nodded encouragingly.

"Oh yes. The boat we want must have lots of stowage."

The cap and eyebrows were raised again. Another scratch of the temple. The officer exhaled slowly, his cheeks expanding. He shook his head.

"A large hold, you say ? Lots of stowage ? Now why would that be ?"

Patiently, they explained that the long journeys they had in mind would involve large quantities of essential supplies. After all, there would be eight of them on board.

The security officer by now had been joined by another man in a similar uniform. George counted the gold bands round the cuff of his jacket and calculated he was the senior of the two.

As if to confirm this, he beckoned at the two bags on the floor and pointed to a metal framed table to their left. As he unbuckled George's heavy-duty belt wrapped round the bag's belly, the other officer continued with his interrogation.

"Why do you need a crew of eight ? She must be a mighty large vessel you're interested in."

As George kept an eye on his bag, rapidly being stripped naked, Colin explained there would be three couples and the remaining two 'crew members' would be under five years old.

The multi-banded sleeves were now deep in George's layers of spare shirts.

"Suppose you give me the names of these three couples ?" The officer drew a small black notebook and pen from an inside pocket. He flipped through the pages until he found a blank sheet.

Colin didn't have a chance to answer. All eyes were suddenly focussed on a large heavy-duty brown envelope clasped in the senior officer's hand. He had torn one end of the envelope away, revealing several thick bundles of £20 notes.

The eyes refocused, this time on George. It hadn't occurred to him that he needed to tell Colin that, at the last minute, Mr Hughes had telephoned and insisted that he be paid in cash. He didn't, apparently, trust banks.

In retrospect, it seemed more likely that he didn't trust

George. It's one of George's traits that he would never dream of cheating anyone, so it seldom occurs to him that anyone else might not be entirely trustworthy, or might not trust him.

He thought the boat seller was just pulling a fast one on the Inland Revenue. While that may not be entirely laudable, it was certainly excusable.

The security officer had spread the neatly wrapped packs of banknotes across the table and was mentally adding.

"£20,000." George saved him the trouble. "That's how much the boat's going to cost." There was a brief pause as the two officers confirmed his addition.

A gentle trickle of ferry passengers was filtering past. Colin regained his concentration first. "Would you mind putting it away again." He jerked his head at the passing line of travellers. "We don't want the whole world to know we're carrying so much cash."

The senior officer turned on his heel. "Take both their names and addresses and passport numbers." He shook his head. Colin was later to claim he had heard him muttering, as he left, about in-breeding and madness being a trait of Channel Islanders.

The remaining officer made clicking noises with his tongue, much like a parent disapproving of a wayward child. He dragged his attention away from the money, staring first at George then at Colin, as if examining the thought processes of the two men standing before him. Despite that he bundled the cash back into its envelope and made a perfunctory effort to fold the end over in a make-shift seal.

At length, and with more head shaking and clicking, he picked up a rubber stamp and brought it rapidly down with a noisy double thump on the top two sheets of a pad of forms. He tore them from the pile and held them out. Like his superior, he had come to the conclusion that he was dealing with a pair of lunatics rather than dangerous criminals.

"I wish you both luck."

The voice lacked the tone of sincerity, but somehow George gained the impression that he meant it.

Safely out of earshot and on their way again, George voiced the question they had both been privately asking themselves. What do security officers expect people to tell them when questioned at Northern Ireland's borders? "We're here to buy a boat and, yes, actually, we're terrorists and we're going to run a few hundred guns into Londonderry ..."

They met Mr Hughes on the quayside in the midst of a sudden downpour. He came hurrying up the slip road from an inflatable dinghy, a denim hat plastered round his head. With a brief "let's get out of this" he led both men to a small bar and selected a table next to a spitting open fire.

The barman hailed him by name as they entered and started pouring three pints of Guinness. Mr Hughes barely looked at him but signalled his presence to a pair of men crouched round the fire. Their walnut faces moved almost imperceptibly in response to the brief nod and movement of his hand.

The drinks in place and wet outer clothing removed, the Irishman duly produced a bundle of dog-eared papers. He took the first three inches of beer from his glass, breathed out with satisfaction and appended his signature to the top two bits of paper before pushing them all across the table to George.

"It's the price we agreed ?" asked George

"Oh yes. Just the twenty."

"And everything's in order ?"

"Certainly it is." The Irishman looked up to view George full in the face for the first time since their meeting began.

Colin picked up the documents and squinted at them in the dim light. Mr Hughes held his pen in front of George, gazing at him with steady eye contact.

"I hope you don't mind, Mr Russell, but I have a pressing appointment to keep." He extended a hand, deeply ingrained with many layers of diesel oil.

George later admitted his hand had been shaking slightly as he handed over the bulging but crumpled envelope. It was quickly whisked away. Mr Hughes glanced nervously about, grappled briefly with the greatcoat draped over his knees and pushed the package into the depths of a voluminous pocket. "You don't want to be flashing that about. You never know who's watching."

George scanned the row of backs, bowed over the bar. Nobody seemed to be taking the slightest interest in anything other than the glass in front of him.

George apologised they were running late because of delays at the ferry terminal. He nodded to Colin, still feeling for his reading glasses. He gave up and put the papers on the table again. He took the proffered pen and signed where Mr Hughes' blackened finger indicated.

"You've bought yourself a fine vessel, George." It was the first time he had referred to him by his first name. "I hope she'll serve you as well as she has me."

Mr Hughes smiled only for as long as it took him to raise his glass again in a brief salute. He poured the black fluid swiftly down his throat and the glass hit the table with a loud crack. For a moment, George thought they were expected to copy him in some sort of dealer's ritual. Instead, Mr Hughes rose swiftly to his feet, stuck out his hand and shook George's and Colin's in turn. With further brief murmurings of "pleasure" and "seein' ya," he grabbed his coat and without bothering to put it on, disappeared into the pouring rain.

George and Colin, mildly stunned, looked at each other then down at the pile of paper in front of them.

"I think," said Colin, "you are now the proud owner of a boat."

George smiled, his chest swelling imperceptibly beneath his damp shirt. He went to the bar, returning with two more pints and they moved to the newly vacated seats next to the fire. It was then that they reminded each other that she should be given a new name. It was at some point during the several pints of Guinness and glasses of Irish whiskey which followed that they decided she would be renamed 'Salamander'.

Around the bar, a few faces, most of them chestnut brown from weather and whiskey, looked furtively round at the two strangers by the fire and smiled to each other. They nodded, needing no words to express their thoughts, and buried their faces in their glasses once more.

They spent that night on board 'Salamander'. Unable to inspect her immediately (as George later pointed out to an incredulous crew, it was dark), they settled down to an alcohol soaked yet still uncomfortable night on the bare bunks.

The first pale light of Northern Irish sun struck them in the early hours of the morning. They woke almost simultaneously and although neither would admit to a hangover, they quickly found a topic of mutual concern.

The spare dinghy, a small generator and various other

minor bits of gear that George and Colin had judged to be non-essential had, by arrangement, been taken away. What they hadn't negotiated, nor expected to find, was a ship stripped almost bare. Even the huge box of tools, left spuriously on her deck, seemed to have nothing to do with her. None of the spanners were of the correct gauge and many specialised tools needed for the engine were missing.

More importantly, George's much lauded winch had dematerialised. Obviously removed in a hurry, the steel bolts that had held it to the bulkhead still remained, scraped clean of rust where the nuts had been removed. A gnarled spanner left at the scene gave evidence to the speed of its flight.

George stood at the centre of the foredeck, looking about him. Periodically, his hand rose as he pointed to the space where some fitting or other should have been. As if controlled by his undulating arm, his mouth opened and closed in silence.

Colin emerged from the wheelhouse, the ship's papers in his hand. Now wearing his glasses in daylight he re-read for the third time the first three lines of the page he had pulled to the top of the bundle. This time, he read aloud. His attention gripped, George listened intently.

"Say that again." Colin started from the top of the page again. "Second thoughts; don't bother."

George and Colin moved quickly, meeting at the top of the gang-plank and almost bouncing each other into the water in their rush to get to the quayside.

They split up, trotting in opposite directions along the dock, peering up alleyways and into the occasional shop windows. Despite their rush, it was a full ten minutes before Colin found a pay 'phone at the back of a ship's chandler. Gasping for breath, he leaned against several coils of nylon chord. Squinting at a scrap of paper, he dialled the number George had copied several weeks before from the classified advert that had lured them to Northern Ireland

The 'phone started ringing and, suddenly understanding, he grappled in his pocket for a coin. He was still waiting when George joined him, pointing breathlessly back at Salamander.

"The radar's missing as well. Let me talk to the bastard." Colin shook his head. There was no reply.

"Well," reasoned George, "he said he was a busy man."

Colin replaced the receiver. "Busy with another dozen pints of Guinness and his next victim, maybe."

Over the next few hours, between cups of coffee and return trips to the chandler's shop, they scanned their papers repeatedly for a clue to the whereabouts of Salamander's former owner. If indeed he was her former owner. All they could say with any certainty was that his name was unlikely to be Mr Hughes.

The ship's papers were in the name of a Michael Paul Murphy and there was a confusing tangle of detail involving some sort of share arrangement with a brokerage company called Thompson, Smythe and Webb of Liverpool.

Twelve calls to the number in the advert failed to reach either Mr Hughes, Mr Murphy or anyone else. They scoured the papers for a home address but found none.

In the small café where they had all but taken up residence, and between mouthfuls of a mid-day breakfast heavy with fat and brown sauce, they searched through a tattered copy of the local telephone directory.

There were two columns of subscribers named Hughes and several pages of Murphies. Sullenly, they admitted they didn't have enough change to feed the 'phone for long enough to give a reasonable chance of success.

They returned to the pub they had been to with 'Mr Hughes'. George asked the barman where they might find the man they had been with the night before. He added what he hoped was a casual lift to his voice. He didn't want anyone to think he was after anyone's blood – nor that their countryman had put one over on him. That, he judged, would only encourage the men leaning against the bar to enjoy his discomfort even further.

The barman and his customers all shrugged disinterestedly. He only called in occasionally. They didn't know his name. In fact they hardly knew him at all. The first time they had seen him was a couple of months before when he started asking if anyone was in the market for buying a boat.

The casual manner was slipping slightly as Colin asked if anyone knew where he lived.

They didn't think he lived locally. He had been staying in a bed and breakfast somewhere. The barman called to one of the men sitting at the far end of the bar.

"That fellow who was after selling his boat; was he staying with Mrs Connolly?"

The man inhaled through his pipe and tapped it into an ashtray, shaking his head. "I thought he said Broom Street. That would be Mrs Belling."

Another, older man, chipped in. "I saw him in Derry Street. Walking down from the top end, he was. That would be the O'Doyle's place."

The room fell silent, the assembly looking down at their glasses, shaking their heads.

The silence was broken by a new voice, conspiratorially close to George's ear.

"He might have another boat along the quay. He could be staying on board." George looked up hopefully. "Oh don't get me wrong. I don't know which one."

Nevertheless, they finished their drinks and walked along the quayside and back again, glaring in search of clues at the vessels rising and falling slowly at their moorings.

"You know." Said George at length, "If he doesn't live round here, it's unlikely he'd have two boats here at the same time, unless there was someone with him. Nobody's said anything about there being anyone else."

They fell to silent thought. It was Colin who spoke next. "There is another possibility, of course." George looked up. By the tone of Colin's voice he was fairly sure he didn't want to hear any more. "He could have towed Salamander in."

They stopped dead in their tracks, staring in horror at each other. As one, they turned and hurried back along the dock.

Reaching Salamander, they went straight to the wheelhouse. George pulled open a steel box welded to the bulkhead and turned a row of three switches. He pressed a red button next to the wheel, waiting for the grinding of the compressor to kick the engine into action.

The engine coughed and the exhaust popped a small cloud of sooty smoke over the grimy water. George pressed the button again, moving the throttle experimentally forward.

It took several minutes and more than several pokes under the engine cover but eventually the beast awoke and roared throatily.

They both sighed with relief, revving the engine a few

times to make sure before turning off the ignition and climbing down into the cabin to bury themselves in thought.

It didn't take many minutes to reach the inevitable conclusion that the illusive Mr Hughes / Murphy had left them no choice. They would read the papers once more to satisfy themselves that nobody else had a clear claim on the vessel then cut their losses and sail her back to Guernsey as she was.

They only had a few days remaining of their holiday; insufficient time, they judged, to track down a dodgy dealer who didn't want to be found and was hiding out in his own home territory.

Even if they did find him, what chance was there that they would successfully negotiate a rebate and still get home in time ?

The following morning, already lamenting the lost winch, they hauled in the anchor chain, hand over hand. They headed out of Belfast, turned south and hugging the east coast of the Emerald Isle, edged through an increasingly choppy Irish Sea.

Colin rubbed Vaseline into his burned hands, their conversation sinking to black wishes for Mr Hughes' future.

Salamander was supposed to have been thoroughly serviced before the sale was completed, but that didn't stop her from quickly delivering a practical joke. A few hours out, just as the breeze and drizzle should have cooled their tempers, the engine coughed momentarily, wheezed and fell silent.

"Bugger." It was Colin who first expressed the emotion felt by both men as Salamander tossed, powerless, between the waves.

George, assuming the role of chief engineer, undid the hand bolts on the engine cover and, for the first of many times, pulled the heavy steel plate to one side. Lying on his stomach, he reached into the oily darkness, torch in one hand, finding his way round the lump of metal he was destined to become so familiar with.

No amount or coaxing or fiddling with its more accessible parts would stir the mighty beast back to life. The radio didn't work and, the greatest ignominy, they had to wait for a fishing trawler to call the Dun Laoghaire Lifeboat to tow them to shore.

Meanwhile, back on dry land, things were no rosier.

Our buyer withdrew his deposit for Carey Cottage and demanded a reduction in the price. In a heated telephone conversation he told me he was disputing the size of the garden. His solicitor had told him, he said, that he must 'clarify matters' with us before parting with any money. He mistook my thoughtful silence for submission and his tone mellowed. He became almost apologetic as he mumbled how he felt obliged to do as his lawyer advised him. After all, what was the point of paying all that money for counsel if you then ignore it?

The amount he was asking to be cut from his original offer was out of all proportion to the slither of land in question, some 18 inches wide.

I was furious. The buyer's mother, who was to be the new occupant of Carey Cottage, had been so eager to move that, from sheer good will, we had already moved out and allowed her to take up residence. To add insult to injury, now happily ensconced in our cottage that her son no longer seemed willing to pay for, she had even complained that the garden was going to be too large for her to manage!

I harboured really thunderous thoughts that, discovering my poor George was adrift somewhere in the Irish Sea, our buyer had taken the opportunity to plunge this bombshell on my doorstep – except, of course, I no longer seemed to have a doorstep.

My solution? I bought a bottle of Blue Nun, grabbed a corkscrew from the kitchen drawer and went to bed. Before long, I felt quite equal to dealing with any number of awkward house buyers, even without my knight in shining armour (or broken boat) at my side.

The following morning, fresh and determined, I put pen to paper. I wrote out a list of all the reasons I thought he was being unreasonable, ending with a thinly veiled threat that the rent we could demand from his mother would more than make up for his wretched strip of garden.

I was just reviewing my list, wondering whether it was too much to include an expletive on every line, when the 'phone rang. It was our buyer. Had I, he wished to know, consulted my husband over his proposal. He knew very well I hadn't.

George has always said that if I have a fault, it's being too open with people we should be wary of. I had already told him that George was stranded in Ireland, fully occupied with his obstinate engine.

I started reading from my list.

"I think you're behaving most dishonourably," I began, hoping the quiver in my voice wasn't too noticeable.

"I beg your pardon ?" He sounded more amused than hurt. I was thrown immediately and abandoned my script. "Well for God's sake, there's your mother, living in our house rent free while you mess us about with quibbles over a bit of flower bed that she doesn't even want."

"Now, Mrs Russell, the price we agreed was for ..."

"I know what it was for – and you haven't even paid the deposit you promised. What if we were to charge your mother rent ?"

"We didn't agree anything about rent."

"But we did agree you'd pay a bloody deposit."

"If that's your attitude, she can easily move out."

"OK then. When ?" I hoped the tone in my voice sounded more confident to him than it did to me. "And what about the deposit ?"

"I'm not sure we will want to proceed with the purchase at all."

"Fine. When is she moving out ? I want our home back."

"Well, fine then."

The telephone was slammed down at the other end of the line. I glared at the earpiece, uttered a final embittered yet ineffectual "right then", and rattled the receiver as noisily as I could onto its cradle.

The local operator, who was known to listen in to as many calls as she could, must have had ringing eardrums that morning.

I gazed at the now silent 'phone for a few seconds before burying my face in my hands. What had I done ? George had just spent £20,000 of the bank's money and I had just lost the only prospect we had of paying it back. I looked at my watch. It was 10 am. Too early for Blue Nun.

From the doorway, two small and puzzled faces peered at me. Still dressed in their night clothes, Kim and Tania had come downstairs in search of breakfast. Kim asked if there was something the matter. Of course there wasn't. I wrapped them in my arms, hugging them close so they wouldn't see the worry that must have been showing on my face.

"Cornflakes or Frosties ?"

They jumped free of my arms, all excitement. "Frosties !!"

Our concerns momentarily shelved, I poured two bowls of cereal. Amazingly, before the girls had finished munching, the 'phone rang again. An altogether more conciliatory buyer had, apparently, been discussing the matter with his mother.

"We really feel it must be possible to come to some compromise." There was a pause. I remembered George's advice: *'if in doubt, say nothing.'* "Mother has persuaded me that she really doesn't want to have to move home again."

I nodded at the 'phone, gathering my dignity. "Well, if you are prepared to be reasonable..."

By the end of the day we had agreed to a drop of £500 in the asking price – considerably less than he had originally demanded – returnable if it was later proved that the boundary line was where we originally said it was.

While all this was going on, our friends proved themselves exceptionally kind, providing us with a roof over our heads. However, as the days dragged on, I became increasingly aware that our high spirited girls needed more space – if only to preserve the sanity of the adults in the household.

It came as a relief to all when George, still stranded near Dublin, telephoned and suggested I brought the children to Ireland. I agreed immediately. It would, I reasoned, be sensible for us all to start getting our sea-legs.

We managed to book flights the following day from Guernsey to Gatwick and were soon on our way, with a connecting flight to Dublin.

The girls were thrilled with all the excitement. A train journey, two aeroplane rides, another car journey, a reunion with their Dad and a new home – all in one day. And a home that was also a boat ! Already their initial tantrums and tears at leaving their friends, and several larger toys, seemed a long way off.

CHAPTER TWO

Getting Nautical

Just a bit dirty !!

They had said she was just a bit dirty ! Which bit had they been talking about ??

Salamander was painted black in places, it's true, but the reason she looked black had nothing to do with paint. There wasn't a square inch of her that wasn't coated in a thick layer of filth laden grease and oil.

Standing on the quayside I grabbed the girls' hands and held on tightly. I had dressed them both in brand new matching pale blue cotton trousers, blue and white striped T-shirts and anoraks. In the spirit of the moment, it had been my attempt to get in tune with the nautical nature of our new lifestyle. As my friend Bill often says, I had been living in a dream world.

I quickly woke up. The dream dissolved. I turned on my heels, whisking the girls round as if they were on a fairground ride, and retraced our steps until we found a charity shop.

Re-decked in faded over-sized jeans held up by snake belts, and with several bars of soap and various other noxious cleaning fluids in my bag, we were piped aboard.

In all fairness, George and Colin had been throwing all their energies at the engine, trying to get it working again. They hadn't had much time to worry about the grease caked over the deck.

For the next week, I scrubbed, scraped, mopped and polished until I reached our living quarters. George and Colin continued to get elbow deep in engine oil (much of which seemed mysteriously to end up over the girls). And as for the girls; my 'little horrors'... they just enjoyed getting as black as they possibly could. For once we couldn't tell them off. It would have been impossible for them to stay clean in the circumstances and besides, while George, Colin and I were black from head to foot, why shouldn't the girls join in the fun ?

We slept in the stern cabin, occupying four of the ten bunks. Colin tactfully moved his bedding into the wheelhouse (it didn't seem quite grand enough to call it the bridge).

By the time we left, we felt we knew the members of the Dun Laoghaire lifeboat crew quite well. They had been more than happy to provide sensible advice and, when called upon, muscle power to help us on our way. In keeping with the grand tradition of lifeboat crew, they had remained unceasingly cheerful, despite foul weather conditions. During the few days we were there, they had been twice called upon to scoop unprepared amateur sailors from the sea.

They had also lived up to the tradition of their countrymen and had been generous with their hospitality, time and encouragement. They had been constantly willing to help and had provided a string of solutions to every problem we faced. When finally we were ready to leave and should have been full of excitement, our joy was tainted by a tinge of sadness.

However, it was a calm day, the engine was once more behaving itself and sunnier seas were calling. When the tide was high, we said our farewells and prepared to unleash Salamander once more on an unsuspecting Irish Sea. A few hours after dawn, George coaxed the engine into life and Colin, now wearing heavy leather gloves, slipped our anchor. We blew two blasts on the dented old foghorn bolted to the wheelhouse roof and edged our way cautiously out of the harbour. George spun the wheel to starboard and we turned south, heading towards St.George's Channel.

The lifeboat crew escorted us until we cleared their coastal waters, finally sounding their foghorn and cheering as we signalled an optimistic thumbs-up. When finally they turned for shore and we had waved our final wave, I repaired to the galley to make cups of coffee. Colin took George a mug to the wheelhouse and stood next to him for a while, gazing out at the grey green sea ahead of us. Half question, half observation, he wondered aloud whether the lifeboatmen's shouts of celebration could actually have been surprise that we had made it out of harbour.

"More like relief, I should think."

The night passed well. Kim and Tania slept soundly and

I woke at around four in the morning to ply George and Colin with more large mugs of strong coffee.

George pointed out to our left at a string of rocks jutting through the surf.

"Lizard Point," he said. We were rounding the tip of Cornwall and well on our way home.

We arrived at Plymouth having made good time and, observing required behaviour for vessels of our size, looked for a pilot boat to escort us in and allocate us a mooring. There was none to be found and eventually the owner of a passing motor launch offered to act as our guide into the inner harbour.

It was now three o'clock in the afternoon and the tide was out. No sooner had we entered the harbour than we ran aground. I'm not sure who was more embarrassed, us or the well intentioned owner of the launch who had brought us in.

The amateur pilot shouted to us that he would find the harbour master and set out in a dinghy. Two hours later he reappeared on the quay, shouting that, because it was low tide, the harbour staff were all taking a meal break. He told us not to worry; he had left a note on the reception desk in the office.

"I can imagine what that says," muttered George. "Please help grounded idiots."

At eight o'clock the harbour pilot appeared on the pier, having apparently found the note. He put his hands on his hips and stared accusingly at us across the water before shaking his head and marching off towards his motor launch.

The tide had now risen sufficiently to give us room to manoeuvre, although in the circumstances we hadn't dared shift without proper permission. The pilot, having approached to hailing distance, must have decided Salamander was some sort of cargo vessel, as he directed us to a berth next to a row of coal barges. Our grimy hull and decks blended in nicely and we didn't feel out of place at all. Seated around the small table in the main cabin, we inhaled the heavy smell of coal dust and tar. George wondered aloud whether we should save the bother of scrubbing Salamander's deck by getting into the coal haulage business.

During the time we had been waiting for the tide to rise, George and Colin had been given plenty of opportunity to discuss their latest technical snag.

Salamander's ancient engine had no gear box. Once the engine started, the propeller shaft was engaged by spinning, either clockwise or anti-clockwise, a small brass wheel that controlled the clutch. Spinning the wheel one way took us forward, the opposite way put us in reverse.

Any vessel with an inboard engine uses its reverse thrust to stop, only rarely being allowed to drift to a halt. This type of lazy manoeuvre relies on the movement of the tide and doesn't allow the helmsman any control over where his ship comes to rest, so for most purposes the propeller has to be put into reverse.

Aboard Salamander this meant stopping the engine, then moving the clutch wheel to the neutral position and immediately re-starting. The clutch wheel then had to be spun into reverse to provide the breaking power. Because the engine was started using air pressure produced by the generator, this procedure could only be repeated four times at most before the pressure dropped too low to re-start the engine. When this happened we had no option but to drop the anchor and wait while the generator built up enough pressure again; a process that could take upwards of 45 minutes.

The knack was in the timing. George had quickly got it down to a fine art, judging our speed and the distance from our docking point to the last second before cutting the ignition, disengaging the clutch, firing up the engine again and putting us into reverse. No amount of practice or expertise can help, however, when the clutch wheel is spun but won't engage the propeller. This had been our problem in Plymouth, discovered only as we tried to manoeuvre into position between two coal barges.

At length, and after several abortive attempts to cure the problem, an engineer was summoned. In the week which followed, between bouts of nut wrenching, spanner hurling and cursing, we found time to greet the arrival of Colin's girlfriend, Barbara, from Guernsey. She had been persuaded it was time she got used to a life on board. If she was to be an active crew member and enjoy our journey south, Colin had told her, she had better have some idea of what she was letting herself in for.

After several days, the engineer emerged from

Salamander's bowels, blackened with grease but triumphantly bearing a lump of deeply scored brass which, he assured us was "knackered as hell." Declaring our clutch problems to be a thing of the past, he quickly scribbled out a bill. The cost of the repair was £200, which we hadn't included in our financial estimates, but at least we could get on the move again.

We were off again, riding the waves south on the final leg of our trip back to Guernsey. On the map, the little bit of blue we had to cross seemed quite insignificant compared to the broad expanse we had already covered.

What the map didn't show us, and never would, was how the weather was going to behave.

The seas decided to teach us a little more of the reality of sailing. George and Colin, of course, needed no telling, but as the waves slapped our bows and a thick fog descended, Barbara and I spent most of the journey being spectacularly sea sick.

My little horrors found the whole experience hilarious and, in my concern that Barbara shouldn't be totally discouraged before she had even begun, and during moments when conversation was possible, I reassured her that if she kept herself occupied she would feel better.

I hadn't expected the remedy to work. Surprisingly, though, she soon regained her normal healthy hue as well as an appetite that demanded several rashers of greasy bacon, fried eggs and sausages. I, on the other hand, partly because I had to produce similar meals for everyone on board, continued to lean over the side !

George's navigation lessons paid off and as we came in sight of our little island I felt enormously proud of both him and Colin. We had planned our victorious return to coincide with a high tide early on a Saturday evening and intended to moor in Havelet Bay where several of our more incredulous friends would have gathered for a drink. They always used the same quay side pub on a Saturday night. Celebration and admiration were assured.

We were already running a bit late because of the fog, but estimated we would still have time to make our triumphant entrance before closing time. Havelet Bay is on the east coast of the island but as we passed St.Sampson's to the north of the bay, the fog thickened.

Colin leant out over the bow rail and, seeing little, waved back to George in the wheelhouse to cut our speed. The drumming of the engine dropped as we slowed to a crawl and Colin strained to identify where we were.

By the time we got to St.Peter Port and Castle Corner, the headland that forms the northern side of Havelet Bay, visibility was so low we almost missed it completely. The sun had gone down hours earlier and, even if there had been a moon, the fog would have cut out its light as surely as it blocked our view of any landmarks round the harbour.

Still hanging over the bow rails, Colin called out to steer to port to avoid a group of rocks. George peered out of his right hand window and spotted them just in time. He swung the wheel round to take us in a long anti-clockwise arc out to sea. George gave the thumbs up sign.

"I know where we are now."

We continued to turn until, miraculously I thought, we found ourselves within yards of the harbour mouth. He later told us he recognised the rocks as soon as he saw them. They were right on the southern corner of the bay and he wasn't likely to mistake them. As a young boy he had managed to run his father's dinghy against them; a mistake that had deprived him of pocket money for almost a year.

Had it not been for George's local knowledge, we might well have gone straight past and ended up in France. I would have said he knew the place like his own back yard – but of course we didn't have one at the time.

We entered the bay and gently slowed. Colin, from his forward vantage point, spotted a mooring point as we approached the harbour wall. He pointed until George waved acknowledgement, then walked back along the deck towards the wheelhouse.

Twenty feet out, George cut the engine, spun the clutch wheel to neutral and immediately pressed the starter. The engine obediently chugged back into life and he spun the wheel once more to engage reverse. Nothing happened. We were still drifting forward under our own momentum and the push of the tide.

Fifteen feet out and George yelled a warning. Colin had already realised something was wrong and was bolting back along the deck. He glanced over his shoulder once more at George's face and understood. He yelled obscenely and at the top of his voice, bent forward and grasped the iron shaft of the first anchor in both arms. With an enormous effort he swung it upwards and out over the prow. George stopped the engine and the night air was filled with the sound of the anchor chain rattling as it was dragged to the harbour floor.

Grunting with effort, Colin hurled the second anchor overboard. Grinding, Salamander's weight strained against the sudden resistance. The chains jarred against the hull. We could hear and feel the decking timbers begin to move as the chains tightened and pulled against their bolts.

With a final vibrant howl of complaint echoing through the hull, Salamander came to a halt five feet from the harbour wall. Colin sat down heavily on the deck, his legs outstretched.

He looked up, his face red and covered in sweat. "Shit, George. That was close."

Standing on deck a few feet behind him, I glanced in through the cabin window and decided not to admonish him for his language. Despite the racket, the girls were still asleep in their bunks, blissfully unaware of the drama on deck. Besides, Colin had confirmed George's confidence in him. He was, indeed, a handy bloke to have around in an emergency. It would have been churlish to tell him off in the circumstances, just because he had allowed a naughty word or two to slip out.

Fortunately, it was by then just past midnight on a Sunday morning and there were few people around to witness our dramatic landing. We called the watch house and, tongue firmly in cheek, reported we had left Salamander in a safe position to inspect her hull at low tide.

"What was that bugger of an engineer's name ?" George asked rhetorically. There seemed little point in checking to see if he had put his 'phone number on the bill.

It was now June and the Guernsey sun, when it put in an appearance, did us all the world of good. We worked hard on our preparations and the combination of exercise and sunshine made us all feel remarkably healthy.

We punted between Havelet Bay and St.Sampson's Harbour two miles to the north in little test trips to allow George and Colin to check out the effect of their work on the engine and clutch and as the whim – and mooring arrangements – dictated.

Rowing the girls across the bay to get them to St.Andrew's School was, at best, hilarious but more often nerve wracking. I quickly learned a variety of deft manoeuvres necessary to avoid the sleek yachts as they slid in and out of their moorings. Altogether easier to predict were the noisy and slow moving little fishing trawlers that still managed to earn their owners a living, plying their trade round the islands. My rowing gradually improved and by the time the school term ended I was proficient enough to avoid being either shouted at or capsized.

Our final two crew members, John and Paula, now came to look us over and, we thought, join us on board. They had heard of our tribulations in Dublin and Plymouth and, when we admitted the extent of Salamander's mechanical problems, it soon became clear they had serious doubts.

Two weeks before we were due to leave Guernsey they finally admitted they were dropping out. We didn't bother to explore their reasons or try to persuade them otherwise. Salamander was a small boat for six adults and two children and she was clearly going to demand a lot of attention. If two of her crew were half hearted about her before even going to sea, they were best left ashore.

That left us with a problem. We had long known that we needed six adults to keep all the routine maintenance under control and to work in shifts when we were travelling round the clock. We would have to make up our numbers and Barbara and Colin thought they had the solution. They had two friends, Zoe and Steve, who they thought might just fit the bill.

We started to discuss their suitability. Were they 'boat people' George wanted to know.

"Well, no. Not really."

"Have they been to sea before ?"

"Not as far as we know."

"How much do they know about boats ?"

"Not a lot, probably."

George and I looked at each other. What, then, made Colin and Barbara think they would be any good ?

"Well," said Barbara carefully, "they're nice young people. They'd fit in ever so well."

"Young ? How young ?"

"Well ... young, you know."

"Do they have jobs ? Can they leave them that easily."

Barbara brightened. "Oh yes. No problem there. No ties or anything."

George was suspicious. He asked what work they did. Barbara glanced at Colin, eyebrows raised in an unspoken plea for help. Colin said nothing, leaving Barbara to find her own way through the argument. She cleared her throat, looking casually out of the cabin window. "She's a dancer and he's ..."

"She's a what ?"

"A dancer... A go-go dancer."

George laughed. I sat, open mouthed, momentarily stupefied at the prospect of a bikini clad go-go dancer going through her routine on Salamander's deck.

"And he's got a paper round."

George's laughter exploded again. "Well, that'll be handy !" He wiped a tear from one eye as Colin, Barbara and I all started to laugh. Barbara covered her face in her hands, the absurdity of the suggestion just hitting her.

"What the hell," said George after we had eventually composed ourselves. "Let's give them a go."

Zoe and Steve arrived the following day. We learned they were not an 'item' as we had first assumed but, as Barbara had said, they had no ties and their lack of experience with anything remotely nautical was amply compensated for by their enthusiasm.

Our daughters, Tania and Kim took to Zoe straight away. She was 19 and from the start was just like a big sister to them. I began to see the advantages of having an extra child minder on board.

And so it was that, just ten days before we were due to depart, Salamander's compliment was completed by an exotic dancer and a paper boy.

Yet again, though, nature played another unexpected trick on us. This time, perhaps I should say Mother Nature; Barbara announced she was in the family way. Suddenly the reasons for her sickness became clear. It wasn't only mal-de-mer, but had combined with morning sickness. I felt a pang of pity. The feeling of nausea and vomiting could make life miserable enough in the early stages of pregnancy without being lurched up and down at the mercy of the sea.

She and Colin saw no problem. The sickness would soon

pass. As long as they were near land, and a hospital, at the crucial moment, the baby could be safely welcomed into the world and, shortly thereafter, to sea travel. Barbara insisted she would have no difficulty coping with a young infant on board. She was, after all, a nurse and had done a course in midwifery. I, on the other hand, remembered only too well the never ending round of night time squawking and sleeplessness. And that was just me and George ! Nappy changing, bottle filling and extra laundry would be more than any of us could cope with. However much I enjoyed her company and respected her judgement on most things, I couldn't find it in myself to agree with her.

I sat her down and adopted my best solicitous voice.

"Salamander's only got a small fresh water supply." Barbara nodded. "We've got just one cold tap. It'll be difficult enough for six adults to live comfortably." I glanced down at Tania and Kim, sitting spread legged amongst a small pile of dolls. "We've already got two young children to look after." I smiled in what I hoped was a look of sympathetic support.

Finally it was decided that we should leave Guernsey as arranged but in six months time she and Colin would return to have their baby on home soil. The decision didn't, of course, stop Barbara from privately disagreeing with me and, unfortunately, our friendship took a severe dent.

Much of their earlier enthusiasm for the venture also disappeared and, it seemed to me, they lost much of their energy to work. Instead, most of their time was spent putting together their plan to get married.

George, ever the optimist, decided everything would work out fine once we put to sea. We had already experienced Colin's help in difficult conditions and this, as far as George was concerned, was evidence enough that he could be relied upon to pull his weight when the need arose.

With the enthusiasm of the new recruit, Steve had already decided to smarten up his cabin. As soon as Colin saw Steve had made a start, his energy seemed to return. He immediately began working on his own quarters, giving it the same make-over treatment. As if in competition, they went at it without compromise.

Wood panelling soon covered the rust and grime streaked hull walls. Each cabin had a sturdy oak pillar which they used to create the look of four poster beds. Eager to keep the momentum going, I lent a hand with general cleaning and labouring work. As time went on, though, and the cabins neared completion, Colin and Barbara's attention returned to arranging their wedding. I suggested a romantic setting on a Canary Island beach, but they had already made up their minds it had to take place before we set sail. Naturally enough, Barbara wanted her mother to be present, but was sure that as she had never taken a holiday further away than Jersey, she wouldn't contemplate a trip to Grand Canaria.

Marriage plans or not, we were determined to leave during the first few days in August. That would give us ample time to get to the Canaries by the end of the summer. It seemed like as good a place as any to spend the autumn and winter while we tested the viability of making a living out of our investment. It would also provide us with a base from which to plan for the following year's holiday season.

We fully hoped that, as George predicted, once we were under way our relaxed and easy friendship would return. George's favourite saying has always been "You'll see. It'll be all right."

Now budgeting for a six month voyage, we worked out that we would need to allow £250 per head for food. We decided to stock up with all the tinned and dry food we would need before leaving and I went ashore in search of the world's biggest supermarket trolley.

I strolled up and down the aisles trying to picture in my mind what six months supply of baked beans looked like. There was only one way to find out. I approached the nearest shelf stacker and asked her if I could talk to the manager.

She seemed confused by the request and, her hand in mid flight clutching a jar of curry sauce, asked if there was a problem. I smiled in a way I hoped she would find reassuring.

I shook my head. "There's nothing wrong." I promised her. "I just want to speak to the manager."

She offered to find a supervisor. With unaccustomed purpose of mind, I told her it had to be the manager. After a minor debate over the capabilities of his deputies, the value of his time, his busy schedule and so on, the shelf stacker disappeared. She returned a few minutes later and I was shown through a side door, up a narrow flight of stairs and into a small room furnished with a desk, filing cabinet and two swivel chairs. This, I was assured, was what passed for a manager's office in the heady world of multiple outlet grocery retailing.

A harassed looking young man arrived wearing crumpled grey flannel trousers and corporate bright blue and orange shirt bearing a name badge that was too small to read. Glancing nervously at me, he took his seat on the other side of the desk.

This familiar environment, apparently, calmed him. After pushing a few bits of important looking paper ineffectually around his desk, he asked what my problem seemed to be.

I repeated the assurances I had given the shelf stacker.

"I have no problem, so far as I know." I smiled in as disarming a way as I could, pausing for effect. "I wanted to speak with you personally because I need your advice." I leaned forward, my voice dropping confidentially. "You see, I want to spend £800 on provisions." As his mouth dropped open, I stroked his grocer's ego, assuring him I had heard great things of his establishment. I had every confidence that he would be able to furnish me with everything I needed.

I thought he was going to fall off his chair. Instead, he leaned towards the door, which admittedly was only two feet away, and craning round to look down the corridor, yelled to someone called Sandra to fetch two cups of coffee. And, he added after a moment's consideration, biscuits.

He glanced at me. I pressed home my advantage. "Chocolate ones ?" He nodded and repeated the order to Sandra.

It was the first time I had actually enjoyed supermarket shopping. And certainly the only time I had received such close attention.

Coffee and choccy bickies consumed, I was escorted along each aisle, the manager at my side, now very much at ease, pointing out his best deals and most popular lines. A spotty young lad was procured from a back room and despatched to trot between us and the stock room, there to haul cases of various confection onto a large cart.

The manager's index finger tapping expertly at his calculator, I waved – rather regally I thought – at the shelves as we passed. Adopting the manner of a duchess ordering Harrods' best caviar, I nodded from one row of tins to the next. Two dozen large tins of Cream of Tomato soup ... two dozen of Mushroom ... ten family size boxes of Corn Flakes ... no, make that Frosties ...

Fortunately, the shop was not far from the quayside and the manager was happy to provide the use of a small van along with two weighty warehousemen to move our supplies aboard Salamander. They carried the boxes up the gangway then relayed them down to George who, by the light of a twelve volt lamp, stowed them in neat rows inside the hold. The grand plan was coming together with such sudden clarity and resolve that, even if we had wanted to, there would have been no chance of backing out now.

One of Salamander's greatest virtues, as George had been quick to point out while we were still deciding to buy her, was her huge cargo capacity. My shopping trip accounted for nearly half of it !

A few days later Colin and Barbara were married. The reception spilled out of the small hotel near the harbour and spread along the quayside. Across and within Salamander her crew and guests swarmed, inspected, discussed and admired the newlyweds' first marital home.

By the end of the evening, confetti, champagne and wedding cake had settled alongside our pleasant, if unconventional, style of domestic bliss.

One final task remained before our departure. I have never liked doctors much. It isn't that I dislike them as people or even that I don't trust them. I have simply been lucky enough to seldom feel the need for them and have always associated them with the misery of ill health. Rather in the manner of a driver road testing a car before embarking on a marathon, however, I thought it prudent to visit our G.P with Kim and Tania. Far better, I thought, to have them given the once over now than to discover hundreds of miles from home that they had contracted measles !

I didn't know our doctor particularly well. He seemed a pleasant enough man and we would nod politely if we met on the street. The last time I had seen him in his professional capacity had been when I was pregnant with Tania. I had waited until I was eight months gone before telling him. He had given me a benevolent but clear ticking off before checking me over and pronouncing me (and Tania) fit and well.

Kim had barely met him. Tania, of course, didn't know him at all – or any other doctor for that matter. Neither of them had any idea of what to expect. He sat in his leather upholstered surgery chair while Tania stood between his knees, watching him with only partial interest. He smiled benignly and lifted her T-shirt to sound her chest. Instantly outraged, she grabbed her shirt with one hand and the crotch of his trousers with the other. Her indignant eyes fixed on his. The doctor's startled expression creased round the edges as her grip tightened. His eyes watered and normal pale colour changed to reddish purple, beads of perspiration appearing across his forehead and upper lip.

Gently, the doctor pulled her T-shirt down again and his voice cracked slightly.

"Let's start again, shall we ?" He nodded hopefully, attempting a weak smile. "I keep a bag of sweets in my desk for my best patients."

Kim tapped Tania on the arm, encouraging her to cooperate. Tania's gaze lifted, her face broke into a cherub-like smile and, much to everyone's relief, she released her grip.

Once fed with sufficient quantities of jelly babies, the examination proceeded unhindered. We were told we were all a picture of good health and with, I thought, a tone which seemed a touch too grateful, the doctor commented that he would not expect to see us for some time. He wrote a note on our papers with a flourish, wished us bon voyage and showed us to the door.

CHAPTER THREE

On The High (And Low) Seas

George's "It'll be all right" wasn't quite living up to expectations.

Our domestic bliss had proved all too temporary. I had waited a long time to get away from the kitchen sink and the oven but now found myself, between bouts of sea-sickness, preparing food for eight instead of four – and, worse still, washing up for eight.

I was on the brink of mutiny when George sensed my displeasure and put his captain's foot down. Between us, we drew up a work roster.

Barbara, Zoe and I were to share the domestic chores and, while in port, the men would do their share of the washing up. (Sadly, none of us were prepared to risk their cooking).

The very fact that it had been necessary to draw up a rota shamed everyone into making an extra effort, if only to prove they were pulling their weight. All, that is, except Colin who, apparently on a point of chauvinist principle, flatly refused to wash up !

It wasn't all drudgery, however. Included on my mammoth shopping list were a few luxuries. I had laid in a large supply of chocolate, mainly as rewards and inducements (bribes) for the children, as well as some large tins of Quality Street – strictly reserved for Christmas and off limits until then. Anyone found even thinking of pilfering would be made to walk the plank before being keel hauled and strung up with the proverbial nine tailed cat.

It was at about this time that I noticed an oddity. Searching for a lost teddy bear, required by one of the girls to ensure us all a good night's sleep, I discovered several Lion Bar wrappers had been stuffed down the back of one of the seats in the main cabin. At first, somewhat naturally I thought, I blamed my little horrors. (Mother's rule: both, collectively, are accused until either – or both – confess).

When neither admitted the crime, and even shed tears that they should be thought capable of such a ghastly deed, I began to doubt my judgement.

Casting round an investigative gaze, I found Barbara, looking decidedly sheepish. Before I could raise the finger of blame to point in her direction, she confessed. It was the pregnancy. Her hormones were all over the place. Cravings had got the better of her. She looked shamefully down at her feet, biting her bottom lip.

"I'm afraid it wasn't just the Lion Bars."

I gripped the table, horrified. My mouth fell open in silent anguish.

I didn't have a chance to ask the question before Barbara nodded.

I found my voice. "Not the..." I stumbled across the cabin and flung open the locker door. Sure enough, the Quality Street tin had been broken into.

Tossing aside jumpers and other sundry clothes left to disguise the scene of the crime, I pulled the large, brightly coloured tin out of the locker. Inspecting it swiftly but thoroughly, my expert gaze took in all the clues before placing it carefully on the table between us. I glared first at it and its broken seal, then at Barbara, intent on rubbing her nose in the residue of her heinous act.

Slowly, I removed the lid and, pulled the empty wrappers out one at a time, inspecting each one with deliberate care. They were laid out in a neat row on the table in front of her. As the trail of wrappers grew and with it the mountain of evidence, her excuses lost their conviction. Barbara's shoulders dropped in submission and her chin wobbled tearfully.

My resolve began to crumble. I love chocolate and always have. It's my greatest luxury and the curse of my life. Every ounce of chocolate seems to put an extra pound on my weight. No doctor, dietician or nuclear physicist has ever been able to explain why this should be. Barbara seemed to sense weakness in my hesitation and, suddenly composing herself, struck at the very spot guaranteed to knock me off my moral high ground.

"Why don't we each have one ? It won't do any harm." She pushed the tin towards me. The waves had been steadily building all day and I was already feeling slightly green round the edges. Resisting temptation had seldom seemed so easy.

"No. They're for Christmas." I glanced into the tin.

"What's left of them. Anyway, I'm not going to put on weight just for the sake of making you feel less guilty."

At that moment, Salamander was slammed broadside by another wall of water and as the table lurched to starboard, my stomach lurched to port. I almost fell out of the cabin and got to the side just in time.

Feeling a little less queasy, I determined to end the argument with Barbara. Our living conditions were altogether too intimate to risk falling out over chocolate. It also occurred to me that if ever there was a time to indulge in all things fattening, now was it. After all, if I couldn't keep anything down, I couldn't put on any weight.

Barbara could see I was faltering. A sheepish smile, normally reserved to persuade Colin to do things he doesn't want to, had crept across her features. She pushed the tin towards me.

I prefer not to dwell on matters concerning my lack of will power. It is sufficient to say simply that the Quality Street did not survive until Christmas. Or until the next day.

Just 150 miles from Guernsey, in the far north west of Brittany, lies the attractive little town of Brest. Perched on the northern edge of a large natural harbour, it's almost fully enclosed and protected from the ocean. It has a long tradition of welcoming seafarers and offering a safe haven from the Atlantic swells. The town's small, family run hostelries are usually full of travellers in need of a few home comforts either before or after crossing the Bay of Biscay.

The arrival of Salamander and her crew, however, sparked off rather a different reaction from the locals – and in particular, the local Gendarmerie.

We paid no attention, as we pulled into the harbour, of the small flotilla of launches that left the southern pier and cut through the waves towards us.

No sooner had we moored than we were surrounded, then boarded by armed police. I don't suppose any of us had been held at gun-point before, and perhaps we shouldn't have been so surprised that we were now. This trip had already provided us with a variety of new experiences.

At the first sight of an automatic rifle, clasped to the chest of the first officer who clambered onto the deck, Barbara and I instinctively raised our hands in surrender. Barbara was later to try and convince us she had only done so in humour to diffuse a situation that Kim and Tania might have found frightening.

Of Salamander's entire company, Kim and Tania were the least concerned of us all, sitting on the deck with a teddy bear on each of their laps, offering each other cups of imaginary tea.

The senior of the police officers flipped his fingers disinterestedly, indicating we could lower our hands. He took a pace forward, his leather boots strangely inappropriate on board ship. He looped his thumbs over his leather belt and cocked his head to one side.

He was a smallish dark man, easily identifiable as the group's leader by the multitude of silver insignia on each shoulder. His small head seemed strangely comical under the wide peak of his cap, but lest we should fail to take him seriously enough, he now stood squarely before us, his cohort of gendarmes fingering their triggers behind him. He spread his feet, now folding his arms, expanding his chest to show off shiny buttons and badges.

He rattled off some rapid French which, I think, meant they had been waiting for us. He hadn't asked for anyone by name and seemed to be addressing all of us, which probably indicated he didn't know who we were. All this seemed rather at odds with the determined nature of their boarding. If the episodes of 'Softly Softly' we had seen were anything to go by, any intrusion executed with such confidence should at least have been accompanied by a search warrant. There was no sign of any such authority here.

Had we been of a criminal frame of mind, I daresay we would have met their advance with loud protests and demands to contact our lawyers. Our silence seemed to catch the invaders off guard, as there was an embarrassing silence while the gendarmes looked to each other for a lead and the officer searched for his opening line of questioning.

George had been born in the Channel Islands and I had lived there for a number of years. Despite the fact that French is as widely spoken as English, none of us could claim to be fluent. In an effort to seem co-operative, Colin asked falteringly what they wanted. The officer indicated the cabin door.

"Please, let us speak English. It will be easier, I think." He ushered us inside and invited us to sit. I have always felt, watching TV police dramas, that when a policeman invites someone to sit down in their own home they are taking a diabolical liberty. Pretending to be the host when one is an uninvited guest can be nothing less than bad manners. However, I now understood why they do it. His simple suggestion made me feel as though I was the one on foreign territory (which, technically, I suppose I was). Convinced that I was a suspect, I knew not what of, it was clear we had no control over our situation – even though we were still in the relative safety of our own home. It also occurred to me that George and Colin were far less accustomed than I was to feeling so helpless.

We all sat, lined up like children on school detention. The large frames of the two senior men in our party were crushed together and hunched forward, their hands clasped together on their knees. Their discomfort was obvious and, I thought, had not escaped the notice of our visitor.

"Tell me, who is the captain here ?" We each glanced along the row of faces next to us. All focussed on George. Nobody had ever said so, but we all knew he was in charge. "Ah." The policeman rose slightly and extended his hand. George shook it politely and the officer settled back again on his chair. "I too am a Captain." He tapped the insignia on his shoulder. "Captain of Police." He laughed as if this was the first time he had heard his own joke.

His laughter turned to a grimace as he realised we hadn't appreciated his humour. He changed tack. He produced a small black notebook from his top pocket and flicked impatiently through the pages. He paused, scanning a page briefly before flipping it shut again. His eyes rose to gaze squarely at George. Why, he asked briskly, had we changed the name of the Deep Diver. George explained we had bought her recently and it was quite usual for new owners to wish to re-name their ships.

"Besides, we don't want people to think we are a diving vessel. We may be using her for any number of other things."

The policeman looked briefly over his shoulder to his heavily built second in command, his bulk filling the doorway. The shadow cast across our cabin table seemed to grow as the larger man squared his shoulders still further. Assured that his reserve force was in position, the Captain leaned forward, his fingertips touching beneath his chin.

"This is what I thought." He suddenly sat upright and snapped an order at the blockage in the doorway. Two more uniformed and armed policemen pushed their way into the cabin. They started opening lockers, pulling out the contents and lifting seat covers.

It transpired that Deep Diver, in her former life as a pirate radio station had been on a long list of vessels whose crews were, for one reason or another, 'wanted for questioning'. Although ostensibly they were searching for illegal broadcasting equipment, I suspect they hoped to find a few drugs as well.

As they ushered us first one way and then the other in order to search the lockers under our seat, they stared, deeply suspicious, at Steve and Zoe. Their youth and several days at sea had clearly given them the criminal look of drug crazed pirate radio disc jockeys.

There was no radio gear, except our two way marine set. The only drugs we had were the bottles of thick pink Kaolin and Morphine indigestion mixture every parent of my generation is familiar with. There were also small bottles of pain killers and sea-sickness pills which several of the officers took turns to scrutinise. The search took almost an hour and they found their disappointment hard to disguise as they finally trooped out of the cabin to await further instructions.

The Police Captain, back on deck, gazed ruefully up at the steel radio mast; the only remaining sign of Salamander's illicit past and, we now realised, one of the reasons for their wasted journey. George shrugged and explained he had sold one mast to a radio ham in Guernsey before leaving home. He hadn't found a buyer for the second one and there hadn't yet been time – or any need – to remove it.

It wasn't only the French police who weren't aware of George's 'it'll be all right' prediction. It was now the beginning of August and our crew was becoming collectively uneasy. We had been listening to news reports about the Fastnet Race currently being fought out over an area of a few hundred square miles to the north of us. A sudden and violent storm in the north Atlantic had caused more damage than at any other time in the event's history. Yachts designed to cross the world's greatest oceans had been capsized and sunk or shattered against the rocks of the

British and Irish coasts. The combined military strength of the two nations' air forces and navies, working with the civilian emergency services, had been tested beyond their limits. Despite several heroic rescues, lives had been lost.

We listened in dumb immobility to our marine radio and the BBC World Service as, one by one, the casualties and missing were reported. Pleas for help from the yachtsmen were promptly answered. Rescue vessels were permanently on duty, scouring the area and hurrying from the position of one mayday call to the next. Whenever there was a gap in the weather, an air-sea rescue helicopter was scrambled. There was talk that the RAF had a Nimrod surveillance aircraft in the area, monitoring the radar and airwaves for distress calls sent out on unconventional frequencies and sweeping the area for signs of wreckage and survivors.

More than once, George voiced the view that we ought to offer our help. It was a suggestion made out of his islander's belief in the unwritten mariners' code of honour. Where a vessel was in peril, it was the duty of every other vessel in the area to go to her aid. Common sense told us that Salamander was not equipped for such missions, and neither was our crew.

The harrowing mental pictures drawn by the snippets of radio traffic and the official 'sanitised' news reports had their effect on all of us. Barbara was the first to admit she had endured enough. Next, Steve reminded us that, although he had conceded before joining the trip that he had left nothing behind in Guernsey, he would still appreciate an opportunity to return in one piece.

Colin's loyalty had to be with his new wife and, once they realised they had all been harbouring the same thoughts, they wasted no time. The three of them left the following day to fly to Spain for a recuperative holiday on dry land. We parted as friends, despite feeling let down and anxious about our onward journey without them.

During our stay in Brest, and every other spell in port, we found ourselves inadvertently entertaining a string of casual visitors. It is a natural trait of most people who live either by or on the sea that the arrival of any new vessel signals an opportunity to make new friends. It was hardly surprising that the boat owners moored along the quay at Brest had quickly noticed our presence, especially after the interest shown by our police welcome committee. The news had also soon spread of the thoroughness of the police search, suggesting we had something worth hiding stowed away. One caller, in particular, George remembers well.

He wore a white cap, greying and frayed from long service, and an equally worn blue blazer. When he walked he had a sort of naval swagger which gave the immediate impression of a man who has spent his entire life on board ship. Either that, or a complete impostor who had spent just as long cultivating a false impression and whose only nautical experience had come from his imagination and stories heard at the bar of his local sailing club.

It turned out he was a Guernseyman and the captain of one of the Dorey ships. Mr Dorey was the highly respected owner of a fleet of cargo vessels and anyone associated with his company was therefore deserving of at least a modicum of courtesy and hospitality from a fellow islander. We were happy to invite him aboard Salamander for a drink.

He certainly seemed to know his way about a boat and, large whisky in hand, was in his element discussing with George the finer of Salamander's details. He praised our choice of radio, recently bought in Plymouth and now lending the wheelhouse a minor touch of modernity.

He tapped the small radar screen and nodded approvingly. Vital, he concluded, in these modern times. The shipping lanes were getting busier with every passing week. George smiled and nodded. He had already told him about the pea soup they had sailed through from Ireland. The old salt's hand went up to his chin. Mind you, there was always room for improvement. These things generally needed a bit of adjustment after they had been installed. You could never be too careful.

He switched the radar on and turned a black knob on the control box. Peering first at the green glass screen, he stuck his head out of the porthole and looked up at the radar dish. He tutted quietly and muttered under his breath, tapping the screen again. That could do with a bit of fine tuning; just a tweek or two.

He left an hour or so later, waving cheerily and wishing us a safe onward journey. I might have been mistaken, but the swagger seemed even more pronounced as he rolled along the quay side. As if in explanation, George lifted the now empty whisky bottle, gazing at me cross-eyed through it before dropping it in the bin.

Not all our visitors were unscheduled. George's two sisters, Janet and Joan along with her husband Eustace were holidaying nearby and, by arrangement, met up with us in Brest. Their arrival could not have been more timely. They cheerfully agreed to crew with us across the Bay of Biscay.

"I told you." said George happily.

"What did you tell us ?" Asked Zoe.

"I told you, didn't I ? 'you'll see,' I said. 'you'll see, it'll be all right.'

I settled down to write a postcard to my Mum who had been patiently sitting at home in Havelet, watching the weather reports and worrying herself sick over the news from the Fastnet Race. She had no way of knowing we hadn't been caught up in the tragedies she had been hearing about.

'Leaving Brest in the morning crossing the Bay of Biscay to Portugal' I wrote without thinking, 'it will take about 48 hours – arrive about Sunday. Janet is coming and Eustace, Joan, George and Zoe.' Fortunately, my card took a few weeks to reach her and, by then, the worst of the storms had passed. Having received no visit from the local constable by the time the card arrived, she reasoned we had probably made the crossing safely.

Another of our regular visitors during our stay in Brest was 'Captain Dan'. We had spotted his boat almost immediately after our arrival in Brest. Named 'The Havelet', it was inevitable that her owner was another Guernseyman.

He was full of sea-faring tales and, unlike the Dorey Captain, his knowledge and love of all things nautical was unmistakably the result of choice rather than a need to spend a life at sea to make a living.

He wore an immaculately tailored navy blue double breasted blazer, discreetly devoid of any insignia. His grey slacks were sharply pressed and he always wore properly approved rope soled sandals. His thick white hair was matched by an equally luxuriant moustache which he occasionally stroked between thumb and forefinger.

He invited us on board 'The Havelet' several times, during which we learned he enjoyed a drink every bit as much as he did a conversation; especially if laced with a maritime theme. We spent several extremely pleasant hours during our first few days in Brest catching up on Channel Island gossip and sharing Guernsey anecdotes.

His boat was a beautiful 60ft. yacht fitted with every conceivable luxury, from the latest navigational aids to a bar that was better equipped and stocked than any pub we had seen. The life sized print hanging above it, however, should have given an early clue to his true colours. The subject of this heavily framed masterpiece was a young lady lying along a couch in the classical style. Only the tops of her pale thighs were covered, by a narrow strip of thin gauze. She cupped one round breast in her hand. Wherever you moved in the cabin, her nipple, and her unblinking gaze, seemed disconcertingly to follow.

The Captain's conversation was both witty and, with Zoe at least, openly flirtatious. It was clear he thoroughly enjoyed entertaining, especially when his party of guests included an attractive young woman. It was quite touching to see how protective George became towards Zoe whenever we saw him approach along the quay side or were aboard 'The Havelet'.

She giggled each time George warned her of his intentions, warning her to be on her guard. Zoe would nudge him playfully in the ribs, calling him "Uncle George" and assuring him she could look after herself.

At some point, I don't exactly recall how, I found myself walking along the jetty alone, carrying two bags of supplies from the local shops. However much food we had brought with us from home, there was always a need for fresh fruit and vegetables. George had gone in search of a ship's chandler and Zoe was entertaining the girls somewhere further down the coast. I passed 'The Havelet' without a second glance, my mind full of problems that required solutions before I could produce a meal for five and still have time to relax on deck before the sun went down.

I was stopped in my tracks by the Captain's inescapably genial voice booming out my name.

"Jean, my love. You look done in." It was a hot day and my arms were aching from the load I was carrying. When he invited me aboard for a drink I accepted without a thought.

I sat in the spacious cabin and my gaze fell once again on the hypnotic eyes and breast of the naked lady. So entrapped was I by her that I was barely conscious that the Captain was holding a camera. He muttered something about "one for the album" and flashed off a photograph of me.

"Do you like her ?" he asked, nodding at the picture. "I won her at a game of gin rummy 25 years ago from a Royal Navy Admiral in Bermuda. A chap called Fogharty, as I remember. Flawless Fogharty the men used to call him, apparently on account of his never having made a mistake throughout his career." He smiled modestly. "Well, Jean my love, I can tell you when he took me on that night, he most certainly made a mistake." The Captain laughed indulgently. "He was heart broken."

He sipped his whisky, pushing his free hand into his pocket and fingering his loose change. "She used to hang in the officers' wardroom aboard HMS Fearless before the last war." His gaze moved lovingly up at his prize and he sighed deeply. "Now, she's my constant companion."

I stammered something along the lines of not being sure she would have been my first choice, but Captain Dan seemed undaunted. He sat down on the sofa next to me, just a little bit closer than was necessary, and snaked an arm languidly along the back of the seat. I shuffled forwards and sipped the surprisingly strong gin and tonic he had pushed into my hand. I was sure I had asked for lemonade.

"You know Jean..." his fingertips brushed my shoulder. I swallowed hard and edged a little further forward, leaning over the arm of the sofa. Perhaps I should have foreseen this. My mother had always warned me about sailors far from home.

"You're a very attractive woman." Well, perhaps I couldn't have foreseen that, exactly. I cursed my naiveté. The Captain was still advancing his campaign, easing his backside a little closer with every syllable. "I know we haven't known each other very long, but... I have become very fond of you, you know..." How on Earth had I managed to get myself into this pickle ? "I think you already know that, don't you Jean... I have such huge respect for you..." How could I have been so stupid ? Now was not the time for analysis. "...Dear George, of course, need never know. I'd hate to hurt the old thing's feelings..."

"Hurt George's feelings ?"

"Absolutely not, my love. No point upsetting the old chap. It'll just be our little secret." The Captain tapped the side of his nose, winking salaciously.

"Our little secret ?"

"Absolutely, my love." He stroked the moustache with Machiavellian relish, edging closer and almost shoehorning me off the sofa completely. He slipped his drink onto the glass-topped table and slid his hand lightly onto my knee. His lips puckered, the heavy moustache moving as if with a life of their own. He blew an exaggerated kiss, leaning towards me.

"Captain, please !" I put my hand firmly on his chest.

Captain Dan closed his eyes, inhaling rapturously. "Yes, my love. I'm impatient too." His hand crept up my leg. I wriggled away, conscious I was backing into a corner of the sofa from which there was no escape.

I didn't know whether to grab his hand or keep pushing him away. I couldn't do both. I was still holding my glass and there was nowhere to put it down.

"Captain ! Stop it !"

"Oh, Jean my love. You are such a tease."

"No I'm not. I'm not..." My words were having no impact at all. It was time for action.

I jerked upright, spilling half my drink over the Captain's neatly pressed slacks. His snaking arm shot up in surprise. "That's it !"

The Captain looked up from brushing his trousers. "What is ?"

"George. I wonder where he is. He'll be waiting for his shopping. I mean, his supplies... his tea... lunch. Whatever. He'll be wondering where I am. Must go." I gabbled aimlessly on, trying to fill the time it took to make an escape. I thanked him for his flattering proposal and grabbed my shopping bags. Bolting for the cabin door I reached the quayside before realising I was still holding a half filled glass. I threw back the gin and tonic, gasped as the hot junipers attacked my throat and put the glass down at the end of the gang-plank just as the Captain's head appeared over the cabin roof, his flushed face a picture of hurt confusion. I croaked one final thank-you and, shopping bags bouncing at my sides, raced the length of the quayside.

I was more than a little relieved when we left Brest the

following day. It was 11th August and by the time the harbour channel was high enough for us to leave, the sun was hovering well above the horizon in a cloud free sky and beckoning us south.

A few hours later, bound for Bordeaux, Eustace offered to take the wheel to give George a rest.

George retreated to our cabin and lay down on the bunk with a cup of tea and a copy of an English newspaper we had picked up a few days before. Half an hour or so later I took Eustace a glass of fruit juice and found him gazing rather blankly at the chart George had left him. He blinked at the compass before noticing me and giving me a reassuring smile.

I decided to look in on George and found him fast asleep, the newspaper spread out across the floor where it had fallen. I didn't disturb him.

George awoke a few hours later, scratched his stomach languidly and sat up far enough to peer outside to gauge the weather. What he saw jerked him quickly into a full state of alert. He swung his legs over the edge of the bunk and stuffed his feet into his deck shoes.

In a single swift calculation, George had accurately assessed the quality of Eustace's helmsmanship. It took him no more than a few seconds to reach the wheelhouse, switch on the radar and pull a large rolled up admiralty chart from the shelf next to it.

By the simple expedient of spotting the coast of France off our starboard bow instead of where it should have been, off the port bow, he had quickly established that somehow (we still haven't worked out how) Eustace had managed to turn us through a full $180°$.

Instead of heading south towards Spain, we were now heading north towards the coast of Cornwall. To add to this momentary inconvenience, the weather had switched from calm sea and blue sky to a spattering squally mess of rain and wind.

George looked at the chart, pencil in hand and waited for the radar screen to display the green glow of coastline that would help pinpoint our exact position. Wordlessly, he pulled the throttle lever back to reduce our speed. Even though he hadn't yet calculated exactly which course we should now take, there was clearly no point in travelling even further in the wrong direction.

The rain was now closing in. It was soon so heavy there could have been a tanker a hundred yards away and we wouldn't have been able to see it.

Although my mind was occupied, feeling ill again, I was shocked at the sounds emitting from the wheelhouse. Instead of the gentle plink plink of the radar signal, all I heard was a string of oaths and curses. Something about a miserable, farting.... whisky swilling.... meddling old....

From that day, our precious radar never worked again. No amount of tinkering, shouting or hitting ever induced another flicker of light or reassuring bleep.

These were the days before those clever little gadgets that pinpoint your position by satellite navigation and George did his best to move us in the right direction by following the point of the compass. The storm clouds continued to gather and pour their contents across our path, blocking out any coastal landmarks. The Bay of Biscay, always uncertain, continued to rise and thrash against our bows. Soon, the winds had whipped up to storm force and each wave that rose up and thundered against us was unmistakably more ferocious than the last.

I looked about the cabin, suddenly concerned that the girls might need some sort of motherly reassurance. They were nowhere to be seen.

I stuck my head out of the forward hatch. To my horror Tania and Kim, already dripping with sea water, were clinging to an iron ladder bolted to the side of the wheelhouse. I could hear what might have been George's voice bellowing from behind the wheel. Although I couldn't make out what he was saying I had a good idea what he meant.

Pushing to keep the cabin door open against the force of the wind, I grabbed the first hand hold I could. We had lashed a rope along Salamander's deck to give an extra grip on the slippery timbers. I managed to get a hand to it and pull myself along the deck to where the children were crouching.

Wrapping one arm round them both and grasping both their anoraks in one clenched fist, the other hand still on the rope, I pulled them towards the hatch and down the steps into the cabin below. They were wet and shivering with the cold but as they looked up into my face their blue lips were smiling. To them, I suppose, the experience had been just as exciting as a fairground big dipper.

The gale continued to batter us without remission for what seemed like hours. Monster waves crashed across our bows with such ferocity that the anchor rigging shifted as we rolled, splintering the decking timbers. Salamander, stoic and broad beamed as she was, drove through those walls of solid ocean as they reared up before us and plunged headlong into valleys of sliding green water. However solid and heavy her hull felt on a calm day, her engine was now screaming in complaint and she was thrown around like a toy.

Partly from shock and fear and partly from routine, I spent the rest of the day being extravagantly sick.

This was the middle of August. The Lord only knew what the weather would have been like if we had set out a few weeks later. We heard on the radio that a large oil tanker crossing the Bay of Biscay had been holed. She had poured tens of thousands of gallons of heavy fuel oil into the sea and was being forced to limp into port. One of her tanks was already full of Atlantic swell and there were fears that she wouldn't make it.

Perhaps strangely, given the fate of this far larger vessel, or just because the alternative was simply unthinkable, I never allowed myself to doubt that Salamander would carry us through the storm.

After a journey well over three times longer than it should have been, within distant sight of land, and for once through no fault of her own, Salamander ran out of fuel.

If our situation had been difficult before, it suddenly became nothing short of perilous. Without power, we rose, fell and lurched at the will of the sea. Unable to ride the waves, George could only steer us, under the momentum of the last wave, into the next. We rolled first onto one beam, then the other. In the galley, cupboard doors, strapped shut with wire hooks, burst open under the weight of my meagre collection of pots and pans as they were hurled about.

A spare cylinder of cooking gas, stowed in the front hold, broke free and, taking the door off its hinges, smashed its way through the main cabin taking two table legs with it. Our one and only mirror, swinging on a short chain, turned its face to the wall and shattered shards of glass across the floor and our store of spare bedding.

It was not until several weeks had passed that George quietly admitted that we would not have reached Spain at all, had it not been for the help of a Scottish tug and her crew.

They managed to come alongside, rising as we fell between the waves. After several failed attempts they managed to get a line to us. They moved forward, tentatively taking up the slack in the soaking wet rope. While Zoe had taken the helm, George had strapped himself to the bow rail while he grabbed the line and tied it to an anchorage pint.

As the tug disappeared out of sight, sliding down the swell of another monster wave, the line was yanked tight, expelling showers of salt water and straining the bolts George had lashed it to.

The cable held and we were dragged, at the mercy of the tug, through the waves. When being towed at sea, the distance between you and the vessel in front is determined by the length of the towing cable. You can find yourself being dragged through a wave, unable to ride over it because your towing vessel is low in the trough between the next two waves.

We finally made land in northern Spain, although it took well over my prediction of 48 hours. Nevertheless, we had much to be grateful to the crew of the tug for. Without their help, we would have been blown in the westerly winds against the coast somewhere close to the national border at the Pyrenees.

We finally dropped anchor in a small bay a few yards from the beach at Puesta de Sol.

The Greek captain of the Scottish tug had been one of those engaged in the rescue (and attempted rescue) of many of the Fastnet yachts. That evening, moored at last in relatively calm water, we relaxed, drank whisky and talked. The three crew members sat with Zoe, showing off their tattoos and impressing her with tales of daring-do. Their captain, meanwhile, admitted ruefully to us that salt water was in his blood. He had gone to sea at the age of thirteen and had, during the 35 years since, spent more time on board ship than he had on land.

It was from him that we learned that one of the drowned yachtsmen was a Guernseyman. Although we hadn't known him personally, he was from such a well known family that few islanders would not have known of him. He had been carried overboard and his yacht and crew all lost. The news caught us all by surprise and left us in silent meditation over the vulnerability of our situation.

The Greek's entire family relied on the sea and it had provided them with a living for generations. His grandfather had been the mate of a barque trading around the Mediterranean and his father a harbour pilot at Piraeus. His uncle had been an engineer aboard a freighter, before being lost overboard on a trip across the Atlantic. His great-grandfather and his father before him had both been fishermen. We all nodded. The sea could be at one moment a generous provider and the next a cruel and demanding mistress.

He looked about Salamander's cabin and patted the inside wall of her hull, still rolling gently in the swell.

"This is a fine ship," he told us. "Old, it is true, but built when ships were meant to take punishment from the sea and to last a long time." He flicked his fingers in the air dismissively. "Not like today. Silly white plastic yachts that snap in half." He shook his head. "Some of them are not fit to be on the sea. They are very pretty, yes." He took a draft of whisky. "But they kill people."

We sat in silence as his philosophy continued. His voice lowered and he beckoned us closer. The experience of the last few weeks, he told us in hushed tones, had taught him a lesson he had thought he would never need to learn. It was an important lesson. He was going to give up the sea and become a bus driver.

We looked at him, taken aback. I thought he was joking, but the sadness which spread across his weathered and tired face told me he was being deadly earnest. He left Salamander a sad yet strangely relieved man, as if a great burden had been lifted from his shoulders. By confiding in us, it seemed, he had made his peace with his ancestors and their great tradition.

That night the sea beneath us refused to settle and, unable to sleep, we were tossed up and down as if trapped inside a manic elevator.

The little horrors no longer seemed to find my seasickness funny. They viewed me more with awe struck fascination. Much of their time was spent in urgent and often heated debate trying to decide how I could eat so little and yet throw up so much!

Despite the appalling weather and other problems, the atmosphere on board was now far happier. Whatever difficulties we came across, we worked together to resolve them without any recriminations or thoughts of whether one was doing more or less than the others.

Zoe was turning out to be a little diamond and although we had offered to pay for her to fly home from Brest, when the others had left, she had very bravely decided to stick it out. We were delighted she had. The children loved her and there seemed nothing she wouldn't do for them – or they for her. She worked as hard as any of us and was also learning fast about handling the boat.

Despite the relief of being at anchor after our journey across the Bay of Biscay, we had little shelter from the elements in the little bay at Puesta de Sol and, having said farewell to our Greek saviour and his crew, we refuelled.

As the fuel tanks had been drained completely dry, George had to spend some time sucking fuel through plastic tubes to get rid of air locks. Once running again, we decided to move on to the much better protected natural harbour at Sada, some sixty miles west.

The weather showed no signs of worsening and the forecast was reasonably promising. At six o'clock the following morning we began to make the run along the coast. The sun rose behind us and, despite ardent pleas from Eustace that he should be allowed a chance to redeem his reputation as a navigator, George kept his hands firmly on the helm until we reached our destination.

Even there, we found that the wind was so fierce we once again feared for our anchor rigging. The anchors were so heavy we had great difficulty handling them, especially now that Colin, our resident muscle man, had left. Whenever we were at anchor and Salamander was pushed or pulled by the tide or high winds, they were of such a weight that instead of being dragged along the bottom, they were more likely to tear the fixings straight out of the deck, particularly after the timbers had been weakened in the Biscay storms.

To save myself from the latest nautical concerns, I decided to put pen to paper before I became distracted by other more pressing tasks. I found a postcard and addressed it to my Mum. *'Now in Sada - very unspoilt, people very friendly and scenery beautiful ...'* I thought it best not to tell her about the storm, the radar, Eustace's detour, our latest mechanical breakdown or Kim and Tania being almost blown overboard. Such things would only worry her.

We left Sada at 10 o'clock on the morning of 28th August. Even though there was a descending fog, the trip went smoothly for once and we chugged peacefully around the Spanish coastline until it began to get dark.

We headed for a small bay and moved closer to the coast. Through the swirls of low cloud we could just make out a large cargo vessel moving gently towards us as we edged closer to the shore. A high cliff rose steeply to our left and we were about 100 feet from it when the cargo ship turned suddenly to shore, cutting across our path. Her helmsman must have known exactly where he was and how deep the waters were. Whether he knew where we were is another matter. George had to swing Salamander sharply out to sea to avoid her. He blew several long blasts on the horn but there was no reply. The ship passed us with yards to spare and within 50 feet of the cliff without a murmur.

We had now rounded the north westerly headland of Spain and at 8.30 that evening, we dropped anchor just off Finisterre.

Relaxing in the cabin with George I handed him a glass of whisky before finally deciding to tell him about my Brest brush with Captain Dan. I waited until he was well and truly settled, his feet up along the cushion of the fitted bench seat.

Janet, Joan and Eustace were on deck with the girls, entertaining them with a game of Snakes and Ladders and Zoe was exploring the shore reconnoitring for a bar.

I spoke quietly, expecting an explosion of testosterone fuelled indignation at any moment. Much to my surprise, and slight irritation, George took the revelation extremely well. So well, in fact, that when I finished talking, he hooted with laughter and slapped his knees as if I had just told him my best joke. I don't tell jokes, and even if I did, this would not have been one of them. I had expected him to be a *bit* angry. Even a twinge of Jealousy would have been OK.

"The dirty old sod !" he managed to exclaim through the laughter. I instinctively looked around for juvenile ears. George choked back another laugh. "He told me he had a woman in every port !" I glared at him as he nodded eagerly in confirmation.

Punishing him, I grabbed the drink from his hand. "And it would have been all right, would it, for me to have become one of them ?"

He shook his head, still chuckling stupidly. "He showed me." He pulled his glass back and took a drink, pointing with it at an imaginary sideboard. "He's got a whole drawer stuffed full of photos. Photos of all his women. Every size and shape, every colour and creed under the sun. And all of them taken with a glass in their hand in the cabin aboard The Havelet. It's the 'Have-a-lot' if you ask me !"

My face must have turned to thunder as George laughed at his own spin on my encounter, oblivious to my discomfort. He rolled on gleefully. "You should have seen them. Some of them were real howlers !" He clutched his stomach, helplessly rolling to one side. He was not helping matters at all.

"And that picture over the bar; remember the one ? The nude woman ?" I folded my arms to send out my strongest signal that I didn't want to hear any more. He was not to be stopped. "He... he..." George could barely get the words out he was giggling so much. "He pinched it from a brothel in Bali !"

I rose to my feet with as much dignity as I could muster and turned towards the cooker. "Get out of my way George. I've got a meal to cook."

He rocked back against the seat, hooting with such delight he was apparently unable to follow my simple instruction.

"George." I stared bitterly at the empty space above the hob, but he wasn't watching. "Get out."

At last obedient, but still gurgling with glee he rose to go. Before he could leave the cabin, Eustace stuck his head round the door, bemused by the unexplained hilarity. He announced we had a visitor. Suddenly sobered, we looked at each other, both assuming the same thing; the Brest Gendarmes had been in touch with their Spanish brethren and we were about to be searched for contraband again.

"Police ?" George asked, instinctively pushing his whisky bottle behind a cushion.

Eustace shook his head. "He doesn't look as official as that."

We trooped out on deck and watched as a small dinghy pushed its way through the shallows and came alongside. It was being rowed by an even smaller dark man with sharp features and black oily hair, brushed straight back from his high sloping forehead. His withdrawn hairline gave his head the appearance of a pair of horns and I immediately nicknamed him Lucifer.

Without waiting to be asked, the little devil climbed aboard and started ferreting about the deck, making an exaggerated show of searching for something. We shrugged and made hand signals, asking what he wanted.

He put his two fingers to his lips and inhaled sharply. Cigarettes. The cheeky devil was after fags. He grinned and nodded rapidly.

We were already feeling decidedly ill at ease with Lucifer who, despite his smiles, was strangely dismissive of our offers of a packet of the finest England had to offer. Waving them aside he continued to pace round the deck, peering first through the wheelhouse window and then into the rear cabin.

More forcefully now, George took hold of his wrist and thrust a packet of English cigarettes into his open hand. He looked down at it, disappointment showing clearly on the ratty features.

"Do you think he wants more than one packet ?" I asked.

George shook his head slowly. "I don't think so. I think the little bugger's after drugs."

"Maybe he is a policeman" offered Janet.

We cast another eye over the dishevelled figure for any clues of his official status. His shirt was pulled out of place to reveal a dark patch of skin, the sleeves ripped and grimy where they were stretched too tightly about his shoulders. His loose trousers, stained with heaven only knew what, were torn below one knee and the waste band hung loosely over a tightly drawn plastic belt.

It didn't seem very likely this could be 'plain clothes' even for a drugs squad officer. Janet realised how unlikely her suggestion was, probably before she had even said it.

Meanwhile, Lucifer was furiously doing his smoking impression, tapping his lips and inhaling deeply. He waved his other hand around his temple, waggling his head about with a silly grin on his face.

"That's it. It's dope he's after. No ! Senor ... No hashish !"

Lucifer looked downcast for a moment, before deciding he had better check for himself and went on another tour round the deck. His loose canvas shoes scraped lazily along the deck as they fell off his heels and he knelt down to peer under a coil of rope.

He looked up at us again, his sharp eyes moving from one to the next as he searched for possible signs of weakness. His eyes paused for slightly longer than was comfortable when he got to Zoe. They looked her up and down. His lips parted in a broken toothed grin and a small pink tongue flicked over his lips. Defensively, Zoe pulled her shirt closer around herself and took half a step back.

Zoe's discomfort was enough. George and Eustace steered him gently but firmly back towards his dinghy and with a bribe of a further few packets of cigarettes managed to persuade him to slither back over the side.

It seemed he hadn't finished with us. Instead of pushing off back to shore, he scrambled back up Salamander's hull laden with a basket of small silvery fish. There scarcely seemed enough meat between the lot of them to make a reasonable meal, but he grabbed a handful and thrust them at me.

"Very good. You eat ... eat ... completo ... you eat all."

Did he mean us to eat the heads as well, we wished to know, pointing at the sad little morsels. Lucifer nodded furiously. "Si, si. Eat all."

I have to admit we made an attempt to eat Lucifer's fish that evening. We fried them in a dash of virgin olive oil and with Joan's best attempt at a tomato and herb sauce. Joan is an excellent cook. Despite the difficulties of cooking on board ship, she had managed to provide us with some memorably splendid meals since her arrival. Lucifer's fish, however, defeated even her. They were so revolting we couldn't even bring ourselves to eat anything else after we had thrown them overboard.

Eustace and Joan stayed up all night to keep watch. If there were any more like Lucifer lurking about on the beaches, we wanted plenty of warning.

We had visions of being surrounded by a flotilla of rowing boats full of little Lucifers, all wanting to trade handfuls of bitter tasting sardines for drugs. Thank heavens he hadn't wanted our tinned food. At least cigarettes were easy and cheap to replace.

The following morning George and I rose early to relieve Eustace and Joan. They stretched languidly and smiled through the sleep that was already closing in on them. Joan apologised that they had used almost half a jar of instant coffee during the night but confirmed the obvious fact that nobody had tried to board us.

I set to work in the galley, intent on providing a good solid breakfast. By the time the bacon had fried, they had both taken to their bunks and were snoring happily.

We left Finisterre at 8 o'clock that morning, despite heavy fog. It was not a good day to be sailing without radar, but we didn't want to risk being visited again by Lucifer or any of his clan.

We had been told northern Spain was not the safest corner of Europe because of the Basque Separatists. Although we weren't actually in the Basque Region, their military wing had begun striking targets outside their own home territory and we had no wish to be considered as a vehicle for their struggle towards independence.

A few hours passed and we had gone barely ten miles when Salamander started her old tricks again. The engine began firing unevenly at first and, while Eustace once again was trusted with the helm, George lay face down on the deck and started poking about in the engine compartment.

She started running smoothly again and, grimy faced, George emerged from the black hole until, minutes later the engine backfired noisily and began furiously to misfire. We steered for shore, George shouting instructions for us to look for a bay or beach to drop anchor. Minutes later, with a final cough, the engine died. We were left drifting once more, still half a mile or so out to sea.

We were too far out to drop an anchor with any effect and, although the fog was beginning to lift, we were now drifting with the tide. This part of Spain's coast was then far more heavily populated by fishing trawlers than it is today, but very few of them were equipped with radios. Despite making several calls for help we received no replies, either from nearby ships or the coastguard.

More hours passed and our batteries were running low. The sun was heading relentlessly towards the western horizon and we were beginning to wonder where the tide was taking us when we noticed a small open boat. She was only a few hundred yards away but barely visible through the fog as she headed back towards the shore.

George flung himself at the fog horn and sounded three long blasts. He took a gamble and used much of our remaining battery power by shining our searchlight in their direction. They spotted us and shouted a welcome back in Spanish.

Hand signals provided all the remaining communication we needed and, following a procedure we were now getting quite practised at, slung a rope from our bows and hitched a ride. Within the hour we were towed into a little bay near the village of Muros and dropped our anchors.

We thanked our latest rescuers with the international currency of alcohol and cigarettes and settled down for the evening. Determined to take a break, George and I leapt overboard and splashed around in the gentle waters until he was clean of oil and I was tired enough to guarantee a night of unbroken sleep.

Engine troubles aside for the moment, we began to enjoy our surroundings. We were just 100 yards from a long curved beach of golden sand. The children were delighted and the following morning, the sun not only rose, but actually found a few breaks in the clouds. We began to remember our reasons for starting out on this venture.

That afternoon, while George grappled once again for his favourite spanner and lifted the steel hatch off the engine compartment, I pulled three deckchairs out of the hold and settled back with Janet and Joan. Tania had proudly announced she had lost her first tooth and, by way of a reward, Zoe had taken the girls to the beach. Peace and tranquillity descended on our little bay.

It couldn't last, of course. It wasn't that sort of trip.

The familiar sound of splashing oars jerked us back to reality. Surely Lucifer hadn't followed us from Finesterre! I shielded my eyes from the sun, now deliciously warm and free of any signs of cloud or fog, and gazed out in the general direction of land.

Sure enough, a small rowing boat was paddling its way towards us. The rotund oarsman, his back to us, was clearly having difficulty. The sand coloured shirt stretched tight across his broad back already had a large dark patch of sweat spreading from its centre.

We decided to ignore its progress on the basis that, thus discouraged, it might go away.

The small vessel disappeared from view below our railings and, for a few minutes at least, we enjoyed peace and a silence only slightly interfered with by the occasional jangle of metal on metal and George's curses from the engine compartment.

The splashing and jangling stopped, which was nice, but were soon replaced by a strange scraping and muffled Spanish voices, apparently registering that the people they emanated from were in some difficulty. Janet and I looked at each other.

I lowered my sunglasses, closing my eyes. "I expect it's just some seaweed brushing the side."

Joan sat upright, looking round again. "I'm sure I heard something. Did you... ?"

"Don't worry." I slid down in my chair. "Just enjoy the – "

"No, I'm sure I heard... Something grunted."

"What ?"

"Like a pig."

Then I heard it too; an unmistakably grunt. We all sat up now. I lifted my sunglasses again.

I was about to get up and investigate when two round and red heads appeared above the guard rail, panting from exertion. They were followed by two even rounder and rather sweat dampened bodies that rolled their way over the guard rail. They lay on their backs, turtle style, apparently unable to move from the deck.

Their grunts now replaced by asthmatic wheezing, bulky stomachs rose and fell in rhythmic waves. The intrusion would have been, at best, a minor irritation but for the fact that these particular bodies wore the uniforms of the Spanish Civil Guard. Perhaps the Brest police had been on the 'phone after all.

George disengaged himself from the engine, relieving Eustace from his duty of holding spanners, and we assembled in the now familiar routine, lined up in front of the policemen. Still prostrate from the exertions of their short journey, it took all their remaining energy to clamber to their feet and recover what little composure they had left.

While they made futile efforts to smooth out the creases in their damp shirts, they happily allowed us to open the conversation with a few initial pleasantries. These dispensed with, they asked their now familiar list of questions. Passports were produced and inspected. Explanations of our departure point, dates and planned itinerary were all delivered without interruption. We omitted to mention the police interest invoked in Brest and said instead that our last port of call before reaching Finisterre had been simply 'in France'.

One of the rotund officers, I had nicknamed him Tweedledum, apparently regaining the initiative after his undignified entrance, started pacing about the deck. He peered through the porthole into the cabin, shielding his eyes from his own reflection. Unlike Lucifer's jerky ferreting, this was an altogether more relaxed, self-assured inspection. We recognised the marque of a well worn police officer's routine and settled down for a lengthy visit.

We were asked whether we had any contraband. I prayed that none of us would be nervous enough to jokingly confess to being a drug smuggler. I had heard of people doing that at airports and being locked up for hours, forced to wear nothing more than a paper jumpsuit while irate customs officers rifled their baggage and sniffer-dogs defiled their clothes.

Fortunately, none of us was in a joking mood. The officers looked first around the wheelhouse, then the sleeping quarters followed by the rear cabin. Here, one of them settled himself at our table and asked to see our passports again. While he leafed lazily through them, rather in the manner of a casual visitor to a library who is only there to kill time, his partner was out on deck, kicking lazily at the hatch to the forward hold with the scuffed toe cap of his boot.

He stared down at the steel cover, sniffed, then laboriously lowered himself to his knees and unbolted it. He lifted the cover. Kneeling on the deck he stuck his head, ostrich style, into the cavernous void beneath. His shoulders filled the opening, and his portly chest became firmly wedged as he strained to get a better look in the gloom. The further he pushed, the more light he cut out and the tighter he became fixed. Bent double, his belt strained against the increased pressure and his huge buttocks shook, squeezing free of his uniform trousers. It was not an attractive sight. Even if his chest had managed the journey, his stomach couldn't possibly have forced it's way through without several months of crash dieting.

He finally admitted defeat and called to his colleague who was by now thoroughly bored with reading our passports and obviously playing for time. He joined his friend over the hatch. Together they stared down into the hold, considering the problem and murmuring quietly, alternately scratching their chins and their outsized stomachs.

An excited argument broke out between them, presumably over whose responsibility it had been to bring a torch.

Tweedledum, the first to have attempted an inspection, seemed to be of the view that there could be something interesting down there, if only they could find a way of checking. Having failed in his initial approach he now suggested, in the absence of alternative routes, that his partner might make an attempt.

Tweedledee cautiously lowered himself, expelling several of the now familiar grunts on his way, until he was lying beside the hatch. With a flourish he pulled a cigarette lighter from his trouser pocket. He shook and fiddled with it until, emitting a small flame, he held it without effect above the entrance to the hold.

Tweedledum was pulling at his belt now, moving it with painful twists of his trousers until he could reach into one of its several leather pouches. Triumphantly, he produced a grey metal torch; the ultimate in search equipment as supplied by the Civil Guard's technical department.

He passed it to his partner lying next to the hold. Tweedledee pressed the switch, slapped it impatiently into the fleshy palm of his hand and gazed into the glass disk on the end of its barrel. He shook it next to his ear, as if this would somehow identify the fault and finally tapped it against the steel hold cover. Nothing happened. With a lamentable disregard for government property, he threw it to one side where it rolled down the gentle slope of Salamander's deck with just enough momentum to disappear over the edge and land with a satisfying plop in Muros Bay.

After making a brief, and dark, survey it became clear that neither he nor Tweedledum were willing to exert themselves further, either to identify or extricate whatever it was in the hold. After a further discussion on the proper procedure, they returned to the cabin.

George had already decided on his tactics. His solution was to first take several bottles of chilled beer from the fridge. As if the officers had made the journey from the shore and clambered on board purely to welcome us to Muros, we toasted their health, thanked them for their visit, complimented them on their efficiency and greedily emptied the bottles down our throats. Once the beer had been despatched, George emptied what remained of a bottle of whisky into eight glasses. We saluted the civic authorities and people of Muros and drank deeply. That is to say, Tweedledum and Tweedledee drank deeply. The rest of us sipped.

Their glasses drained, and as if in answer to our next question, Tweedledee picked up one of the passports and assumed an expression of concerned doubt. He shook his head, inspecting the page closely.

Whispering in her ear, George gave Kim, who had now returned from her visit to the beach, some instructions. She was carrying a plastic bucket full of shells, harvested from the sands. Slightly reluctantly, but realising she wouldn't be able to carry it and complete her mission she put it on the table. Eyeing the two policemen suspiciously, certain they were going to confiscate them, she retreated backwards towards the deck.

Whether the officers knew it or not, the hold which they had so miserably failed to infiltrate and which Kim was now slipping easily into, was jammed full of booze. I had already expressed my concerns to George that any visiting customs officers would quickly decide we were 'booze cruisers' and squeeze us for all the excise duty they could get.

The fat twins' eyes positively stood out on stalks at the sight of a fresh bottle arriving and their glasses were quickly offered up and refilled. Seeing an end to our dilemma, George suggested they might keep the rest of the bottle. He felt sure they would deserve a drink after their day's work. They nodded sagely.

After what seemed an appropriate pause (sufficient for several more glasses of whisky) George asked if all was in order with their passports. Tweedledum nudged Tweedledee and nodded towards the bottle.

"Ah, si. All is in order, I think. If..." He tapped the bottle with the back of his index finger. "You understand?"

We understood. Kim went back to the hold. At the arrival of the next bottle the exaggerated and vexed expression on the officers' faces turned immediately to one of confidence and reassurance. The tubby twins smiled at each other and at the assembled company, like the Cheshire Cat they presumably had waiting for them back in Wonderland.

"It will be..." the policeman searched for the words "...all right."

I thought that was George's line?

The twins finally rolled over Salamander's guard rail and, somehow, managed to land in their rowing boat. The prow rocked under their weight, diving briefly below the surface and soaking their boots in sea water.

The last I saw of them, Tweedledee was standing unsteadily at the front of the boat, waving his arms like an uncoordinated windmill and trying to keep his balance on the millpond calm bay. Tweedledum was sitting heavily at the back, his backside being splashed as the water lapped over the side. He was struggling with the oars while clutching his whisky bottle under one arm and waving madly at Tweedledee with the other, imploring him to sit down before he capsized them.

George led me gently away from the guard rail preferring not to watch as they unsteadily made their way to shore. Neither of us relished the prospect of having to rescue two fat and very drunk policemen. Instead, I occupied myself with the washing up and rehearsing my evidence to the coroner's court.

"I didn't see what happened my lord... No, of course we didn't ply them with alcohol and set them adrift in an open boat."

The following day we were awakened by a sudden and ear shattering clatter and roar of engines. The local fishing fleet had arrived the previous night and at four a.m were starting off on their next day's work. They swarmed about us like a school of baby fish, noisily winding up anchor chains, shouting greetings to each other and generally disturbing the peace.

We were to discover that fishing is one of the very few industries in the area, so it would have been unfair (and quite pointless) to complain.

We took the children to the beach again. They deserved all the holidaying they could get after what we had been through. I went off to Muros in search of fresh fruit for our breakfast. Corn flakes are all very well, and however much I dislike cooking, I conceded that we needed fresh provisions from time to time, even if they included a few eggs which invariably required a bit of work before they were fit for consumption.

The village was a real picture postcard sort of place. The tourist trade hadn't yet got its tentacles into the area and, apart from the occasional battered car, it was clear that this little bit of Spain had barely changed during the last few hundred years.

Amongst the throng of elderly widows, clad entirely in black and clutching their cane baskets or, occasionally, a live chicken held upside down by its legs, we were easily identifiable as being among the few visitors to their village. To these occasional intruders, the locals were happy to nod politely as they passed.

The houses were little more than stone shacks, their curved terra-cotta roof tiles held down by judiciously placed rocks. Despite their primitive state, all were brightly whitewashed and, where I could steel a furtive glance through an open doorway, were kept meticulously neat and tidy. A tiny 14th century church, Santuario de la Virgen del Camino, stood in the middle of the village. Despite the almost subsistence level of their existence, the villagers had obviously looked after it well over the centuries. There wasn't a loose bit of plaster or an inch of unpolished wood in sight. Inside, another of the ubiquitous black widows was on her hands and knees scrubbing the stone floor. The brass ornaments, like the wood, was all spotlessly polished, reflecting the daylight that streamed through the rainbow of stained glass. Like the rest of Muros, it was immaculately cared for.

As if to complete the picture, nature had surrounded the village with rolling hills. The peaks of the Cantabrian foothills, hazy and purple grey in the distance, were lightly topped by a few fleeting white clouds on a sky of pure azure blue.

We wandered along the idyllic beach, our shoes in our hands and trouser legs rolled up, kicking the soft sand with our toes. Zoe chatted happily about what she would like to do when we reached the Canary Islands. Janet, Joan and Eustace conceded that, had they not had work commitments, they might have liked to come with us, especially now the weather had improved. I contemplated the possibility that I might be able to buy chocolate soon, our supply of Lion Bars and Quality Street having long since expired.

Kim and Tania splashed along by the water's edge, their happy self-sufficient ability to play restored once more. Perhaps we would stay here a few days longer.

Suddenly, Kim let out a loud shriek, closely echoed by Tania. Wide eyed, they started jumping and hopping in the shallow water, lifting their knees high. Zoe and I turned as one and ran to them, splashing clumsily through the surf.

Together, we saw what the commotion was about and we too began the frantic shrieking and hopping dance. Floating on the surface of the water, their spidery legs spinning like tiny uncontrollable paddles, hundreds of minute red crabs swam and nipped at our invading feet. Zoe and I grabbed one girl each and jumped as hard as we could towards the dry sand. Paradise lost, we ran as fast as we could back to Salamander, leaving Eustace, Janet and Joan looking curiously down at the swarming crabs from the safety of the dry sand above the high-tide mark.

It was here in Muros that we discharged our temporary crew. Now experienced sea-farers and no longer the strangely green hue they had been a few days earlier, they professed a reluctance to continue their journey on dry land. Land somehow didn't seem likely to yield the excitement of the sea. They agreed the trip had been totally unforgettable and that they had gained a valuable education. George went with them by taxi to the railway station and saw them safely on board a north bound train. He wouldn't let Eustace forget his time at Salamander's helm and insisted on giving him a small pocket compass as a keepsake.

However peaceful and ordered our life was becoming in Muros, the weather soon showed it was still in charge. Apparently we had been given our ration of calm seas and sun. By our third day the winds had picked up again and even our little haven of a bay was getting choppy. As if bored by our presence the elements were now showing signs of irritation that we hadn't moved on.

It was now Saturday and, taking the hint, we began contemplating a move. Bearing in mind our crew had now been reduced to three, we would only be able to travel throughout a full 24 hour day if the weather conditions became really easy. With the memories of our mechanical problems still fresh in our minds, we didn't want to go too far from land. Neither did we want to find ourselves stranded in an area where there was no other shipping to help us out. Given all these limitations, we decided it would be better to avoid travelling on a Sunday when most fishing vessels, we assumed, would be taking a day off. The decision was made and we settled down for a further 48 hours of continued tranquillity before our next move.

I don't know whether George or I heard it first. All I know is that I screamed; an uncharacteristic reaction, even in extreme circumstances. George cursed and, I'm sure, shouted "take cover," or something of the sort. Of course, he denies that now.

Either way, we fell out of our bunks, foolishly ducking below the level of the port-hole. It took us a few seconds to establish it was just after 4 o'clock in the morning and we had been jolted into life by a series of loud explosions. As another explosion rattled every piece of glass and crockery on board, George crawled to the door and looked outside.

Surprisingly, everything seemed to be intact. It was perhaps a measure of what we had begun to expect that we had simply assumed someone was trying to blow us out of the water. Another explosion, and we managed to get some bearing on where they were coming from. A cloud of dust and smoke rose from a point high in the hills above the beach. Someone was either playing free and loose with charges of dynamite or firing an extremely large cannon. If not, it was the biggest fireworks party since Guy Fawkes had ensconced himself under the Palace of Westminster.

We discovered some hours later that Sunday was their day for blasting large areas of their local mountain away. The industries of Muros, we should now note for future generations of unsuspecting tourists, include fishing and copper mining.

The Sabbath, I had always assumed, in traditional Catholic countries, was spent quietly in church or cooking vast family meals, just as in more agnostic nations it is spent mowing lawns and washing cars.

After half an hour or so it became clear the blasting would make further sleep impossible. The wind was picking up and, before it became impossible, we decided to take the girls ashore and allow them to burn off their excess energy on the beach. As had become my routine, I packed a few snacks, a bar of soap and a bottle of shampoo before we left.

Before long we became quite accustomed to the explosions and the girls didn't even look up from their game as each successive ton of mountain was blown away. We had been on the beach a little more than an hour and the wind was gusting around the headland. I had washed Tania's hair in the sea and was just doing Kim's when I heard a familiar voice shouting above the rush of the tide. I turned to see George, leaning over Salamander's prow, waving wildly with both arms. He beckoned urgently.

Then I saw why. Salamander was drifting. Slowly but surely, the tide, high winds and the action of the waves had dragged her against the great weight of her anchors. Pulling at the ancient bolts the timbers had begun to creak until George, playing it safe until we could make some repairs to reinforce the deck, had hauled one of the anchors free of the sea bed. Now the second anchor was being dragged through the soft sand. Behind Salamander, the rocks which surrounded the bay loomed large. If he didn't get her engine started quickly and move to a more sheltered position, she would be pushed onto them – or anywhere else the tide wanted to push her.

We ran back to the dinghy and I rowed as hard as I could. All that practice in Havelet Bay was paying off but it still seemed that for every yard I made, Salamander retreated another yard from us.

As ever, the little horrors thought it was great fun and urged me on with shouts of encouragement, beating out the rhythm of the strokes on the sides of the dinghy.

There comes a time in every parent's life when, with slight feelings of guilt, they begin to wish their children had turned out differently. Why couldn't I have two strapping teenage sons instead of two young daughters ? Strapping teenage sons are noted for rowing their mothers around Spanish bays in high winds. Life could have been so much easier !

My hands rubbed raw and arms aching, we eventually managed to get alongside Salamander, miraculously still in one piece, and clambered aboard. George started Salamander's engine and swung the wheel round to point us out to sea. We beat the tide and moved her further round the bay to shelter from the worst excesses of the weather but the high winds marked the end of our opportunity to relax. We stayed awake through the next night, watching and listening to make sure the anchors didn't drag again.

The following day, the wind continuing relentlessly to rock us at our mooring, we scanned our charts for any sign of a harbour that might afford more protection. It was uncanny how, even in this little bay, the wind still managed to find us. It was as if vast fingers spread and explored every cove and cranny of coastline until they found us, then, playfully almost, flicked and slapped at the surface, throwing us about on the water.

Vigo seemed the best bet. It was a larger town than Muros and sat on the southern shore of a long inlet. If we could get far enough into this natural harbour we would be protected from all but the strongest westerly winds.

Our problem was that it was a good forty miles away. If we left straight away, we would be lucky to get there before nightfall. We could see from the charts that the stretch of coastline between us and our destination was sprinkled with rocks and narrow coastal channels. George predicted they would create sharp currents and there were whole areas of sandbars and shallows. We would have to avoid them all, he explained, by sailing at some distance from the coast. Importantly in these weather conditions, they blocked any quick route to a secure landing point should we run into trouble along the way. With only three adults and two young children on board, the conditions were becoming too severe to make the move. We would just have to sit it out and wait for the weather to break.

The next day was 4th September. We had had little or no sleep for the previous two days and nights and were getting uneasily accustomed to being bounced around like a cork. With a degree of resignation I began to understand why Colin, Barbara and Steve had decided to leave.

Suddenly and quite eerily, at 3.30 that afternoon, the winds dropped and our little bay once more took on a sheen of tranquil calm. Seated on the deck in the afternoon sun it was hard to believe that it had ever been otherwise.

At 6 o'clock that evening, gazing out to the western horizon from the stern guard rail, I saw something moving in the water which made me call George, Zoe and the children to where I was standing. I pointed, and as their eyes followed my finger out to sea, I heard the girls inhale a sudden breath of surprise.

Fifty yards out, sleek and silver grey, we saw our first school of dolphins. A small group were leaping from the calm waters of the bay. Gradually they closed in until they were circling inquisitively around Salamander. Their streamlined bodies arched out of the smooth waters and back without a ripple. I knelt down beside my girls and explained they had come to welcome us to Spain. Tania looked at me questioningly. Before she could ask, I told her they hadn't come before because the sea had been too rough. They prefer the calm weather. The girls nodded wisely and we gazed in wonder at one of nature's greatest achievements.

Kim slipped her small hand into mine. "I prefer calm weather too."

Don't we all, I thought.

Ever practical, George had been more occupied by thoughts of how to make our position safer. He had decided we had to do something about our anchors. They each weighed $4^1/_2$ cwt. They were too large and heavy for us to handle and for the damaged deck around their fixing bolts. The following morning, he set out on a bargaining expedition and rowed round the harbour in search of a trade. He eventually identified a likely candidate; a vessel slightly larger than Salamander but with two smaller anchors. After much bartering he successfully reached an agreement and we made the exchange, refilling our water tanks as part of the deal.

At one o'clock the next day, beneath a still and cloudless sky, we left Muros on a dead calm sea.

We made good headway, but within a few miles ran into a bank of thick fog. With no wind to clear it we had no choice but to plough on and hope to find clear weather on the other side. George stood forward on the deck, sounding the fog horn. We managed to safely negotiate the mouth of the Tambre Estuary, identifying our exact position from village landmarks and the coast road. We continued south towards Vigo. As the fog was slowly burned away, the sun broke through the clouds and the forty mile journey seemed far less daunting. If the weather held, we decided, we could carry on, by-passing Vigo and heading for a more southerly port, perhaps as far as Portugal.

By the time the sun slowly dipped behind the vast Atlantic, and the weather still holding, we tuned in to the BBC World Service. The weather forecast was clear and calm. We took turns through the night, two on duty while one slept, until once again the sun reappeared over the Spanish mountains.

We were at last making good headway and thoroughly enjoying ourselves. We waved cheerfully at passing fishing boats as they headed out in the honey light of the early morning sun. There is an unmistakable camaraderie in the common purpose of people at sea. Those who through circumstance or choice take their chance with the oceans clearly understand the need to look out for each other. During an era when this was not always apparent on land, it was reassuring to be surrounded by seafaring folk.

Becoming ever more accustomed to our environment and perhaps for the first time since leaving Ireland, I felt at one with nature. This is how I had always envisaged our life on board should be.

The smooth waters were once again our freshly surfaced highway while the gentle Spanish coast provided an ever changing variety of scenery. Like a film, projected onto a vast panoramic cinema screen, we watched as a long flat beach appeared, the lives of its inhabitants being acted out before us. Small children played in the shallows while fishermen pottered about in their boats, pulling at their nets or sitting around, we imagined smoking and chatting in the warm sun. Minutes later the beach had gone, replaced by rolling hills and grey mountains. Occasionally a small car or van would play hide and seek between the trees, moving silently along an invisible coast road or a train would slide by, hissing in and out of the long early morning shadows. We waved at nobody in particular, knowing we were too far out to be seen.

We were making slow but steady progress. Salamander was behaving herself, the low drum of her engine reassuringly regular below our feet. All was well with the world. By the time I started preparing a meal and glanced at the map we had passed Vigo. The Spanish mountains had first shrunk into hills and now had given way to the long smooth coastal plain of Portugal, spreading out off our port bow. The next natural harbour was Aveiro, some 60 miles south.

The children lent over the prow with Zoe, all three wearing just T-shirts and shorts for the first time in days. They clutched her hands, laughing at some joke or other and pointed. They shrieked with delight at ripples, they insisted, could have been dolphins, flying fish or mermaids.

It couldn't last, of course. It still wasn't that sort of trip.

As afternoon came, the sun disappeared, embedded in thick cloud. Out came the jumpers again. The girls' shorts were replaced by jeans and we ploughed into a bank of fog once more. This wasn't like the half hearted misty efforts we had encountered further north. This was heavy and dense; so thick you could almost taste it. I hadn't seen fog like this since I had visited friends in London almost twenty years before. In those days it was called smog and each time it descended, it stopped the world in its tracks.

I moved to the front of the deck and joined Zoe and the girls. They were already making a game of it. They waved their hands in the air to make smoky changing patterns, identifying faces in the clouds. I extended my arm to join in and realised with silent disquiet that I couldn't see beyond my hand.

By evening, visibility had dropped to below two feet and George had slowed Salamander as far as he dared without stalling the engine. We sounded the foghorn and peered pointlessly out over the sea.

As I stood at the prow, in the wheelhouse George watched the compass uncertainly and cursed once more the silent and redundant radar. The movement of the deck told us we were heading back into rough weather. He called forward to me, asking what I could see. I shouted back.

"Nothing, George. Nothing at all." I strained my eyes in the direction of where I thought there might be a bit of land, a lighthouse even, from which we might identify our position and judge our distance from the shore. George called me back to the wheelhouse and described his plan of action.

We would carry on slowly, feeling our way until nightfall. Then, if we couldn't pick out any landmarks from lights along the shore, we would edge our way closer to shore. If necessary we would take depth readings with a plumb line until we found some shelter to drop anchor for the night.

I nodded in agreement and moved back towards my position as look-out.

Suddenly, sickeningly, Salamander's hull resonated with a grinding, wrenching shudder as she touched bottom. George spun the clutch wheel back, stopping the engine and re-started her, throwing the engine into reverse. The engine roared in protest, too late.

Salamander was stuck fast, her keel well and truly embedded; entangled in sand and sea bed.

As if to confirm our greatest fear, she shuddered briefly then slowly, so slowly, began listing to starboard. George switched off the ignition and ran from the wheelhouse, slipping on the wet planks of the deck, shouting at us to answer him.

His shouts were cut short as he lost his footing and landed heavily on Salamander's timbers. His shin caught the edge of a piece of winding gear and he cried out, cursing.

Up until that moment I had never heard George utter so much as a hint of panic. Now he was shouting frantically at the top of his voice, his only means of finding us.

I called out in reply, asking if he was all right then, without waiting for a reply, screamed at Zoe to hang on to the children. I slid down the increasing incline of the deck. I already knew we were going overboard. I reached into a locker and pulled out all the life jackets we had. Quickly, I threw one towards the sound of Zoe's voice. My first priority was to make sure the girls would float. I grabbed a shadow in the mist, which turned out to be Kim, and pushed a second life jacket over her head. Zoe called out that she had put the other one on Tania. I was a strong swimmer and was confident I wouldn't need one. There was a creaking noise somewhere far beneath us and we felt the deck keel further to one side. There was still one life vest left over. I climbed up the slope of the deck, nearly tripped over Tania, and pulled it round her, tying the nylon chords tightly round her waist.

To this day, Kim swears I must love Tania more than her because she was the one I put the second life jacket on. The truth is, Tania was younger and the weaker swimmer of the two. Having said that, I don't recall being able to consciously apply logic or analyse the risks. I just grabbed the nearest child and made sure she wouldn't sink !

I reached into the locker again and pulled out a distress flare. George had now arrived, clutching his shin and looking pointlessly down over the side. He glanced round at me, then at my shaking hands clutching the bright red cardboard tube.

"Do you know how to work that bloody thing ? Read the instruct –"

"I'm not that thick." I said indignantly. Besides, this was no time to go over our sailing lessons again. "Of course I know how to use it. You just pull on this ring..."

I pulled. The flare crackled. A bright light flashed. The detonator shot a ball of white-hot flaming chemicals from the end of the tube – straight into George's foot. I had been holding the damn thing upside down !

George hopped furiously about, shaking the last of the molten magnesium from his canvas shoe moments before it ignited, sizzling into the sea.

He clutched his smoking foot and, momentarily speechless, glared at me with a cross between horror and disbelief. As if disposing of incriminating evidence, I threw what remained of the smouldering tube overboard. "All right, I know," I told him. "You live and learn."

The air turned blue as he found his voice and gave vent to his darkest thoughts. He didn't seem very receptive to my home-spun philosophy and it didn't seem the right moment to admonish him for his language. As the girls gazed up at their father in silent wonder, he limped off to untie the dinghy.

While I worried over George's foot, albeit from a safe distance, Zoe took a firm grip of the situation. She scooped the girls up, one under each arm, and followed George up the deck. She sat them both down at the front of the dinghy. Still muttering, George lowered it over the side, Kim and Tania already enjoying the ride. Zoe and I clambered over the side after it and I took up my position on the rowing seat, aiming us towards what I hoped was the shore.

I gave a few hefty pulls on the oars, making headway. The third time they dipped below the water, they hit something solid, jumping out of the rowlocks. I struggled to reposition them, pushing down to lift the blades. Suddenly finding no resistance, and adrenalin pumping, I fell backwards, sending the oars skittering over the surface and upwards, showering Zoe with salty foam.

Dripping from her seat in the stern, she wordlessly shook the drops from her eyes and leaned out over the side. Her arm plunged into the sea, reappearing with a handful of sand.

I pulled the oars on board and gingerly stood up. Instructing all three of my charges to stay put, I stepped over the side and into the water. It reached just below my knees. Wading a few steps, the bottom sloped sharply up and, within a few yards, I found myself standing on dry sand.

Paddling, I pulled the dinghy a few feet up the beach and while Zoe and the girls disembarked, waded out to Salamander. Looking up, I saw George, silhouetted weakly against a moonlit cloud background. I called his name.

"What the Hell are you doing there?"

"George, we're right on the beach."

"Bloody Hell."

"It's all right. The girls are safe. We're all OK."

"Bloody Hell." He slumped forward over the rail above me, dropping his head onto his forearms. "I though I was out on a sodding sand-bar!"

George climbed over the side, lowering himself from the lower edge of the deck and allowing himself to fall the remaining few feet into the water beside me. Almost as soon as we waded ashore, the fog started to lift. We found we were on a long beach of smooth golden sand which already was beginning to fill with small groups of people.

The groups merged together and became a crowd, inquisitive and pushing, curiosity impelling it forward. As the dusk gathered to replace the fog and the tide slowly receded, we began to make an assessment of the damage. All around us were large and irregular grey rocks. Poking through the sand like the teeth of a rusty half buried saw. It was as if they had been waiting for us, the unaware and unwary. By pure chance we had beached between them.

It seemed, in this cold grey light, that Salamander's hull was intact.

CHAPTER FOUR

Shipwrecked !

We stood, knee deep in sea water, and gazed up at Salamander's great timber bulk, now towering forlornly above us.

"We'll have to wait for the next high tide," George suggested. I looked around. As ever, Zoe was watching over the girls. They were already happily running up and down the beach in the fading light and with a growing following of local children chasing and shouting happily after them as if this were all part of their daily routine.

They paused occasionally to stoop and pick up shells or pebbles, inspecting them briefly and consulting their new friends before throwing them away and running on. To anyone new to the scene, had it not been for their life vests, they would have seemed to be a pair of normal holidaying children enjoying the end of a carefree day.

The tide had withdrawn another few yards and George rolled up his trouser legs. Pointlessly, I thought as he was already soaking from the waist down. He waded out and bent double to inspect the deeper reaches of Salamander's hull. When he straightened up again, I could tell we had serious problems.

The propeller was deeply embedded in the sand. There was no way of telling what damage it had sustained until she was afloat again. He wiped grit and oil off his hands on a rag he habitually kept in his trouser pocket before rubbing the back of his head. At worst, the propeller shaft might be bent or broken. If so, it would mean a hefty bill.

The sun was now going down and despite the gathering gloom, the crowds showed no signs of dispersing. They had started their own inspection of the damage, exchanging expert opinions and either laughing or shrugging and shaking their heads. They had quickly learned we were English (we had long before given up trying to explain the difference between Guernsey and England). This, albeit inaccurate, identification seemed to have gone a long way to explain our predicament.

Each of them, as if waiting their turn, approached George to deliver their opinion in rapid Portuguese. They pointed to various bits of sand covered keel, rudder or propeller, then above their heads to the hull. They gestured with open palms and raised shoulders. They patted the sand, pointed to the horizon and shook their heads. They mimed pulling an imaginary rope in a tug o' war competition and pushing against an invisible wall. They knelt down and slid their hands along the wet surface of sand. To each of these impenetrable pantomimes, George nodded and rubbed his chin.

One of the locals, however, standing silently and slightly apart from the others, simply waited. Only when all the others had spoken their piece and wandered away did he eventually approach George. He told him quietly and in native English, coloured only by a slight west-country burr, that it was most unlikely we would be re-floated by the tide.

George asked him why. The newcomer, who introduced himself as Yorkie, explained that this had been the highest tide the west coast of Portugal had seen for a century. It had been the result of a combination of high winds, low pressure and the aspect of the moon. The sea may never again, during our lifetimes, become so deep around Salamander's hull.

Yorkie gave a huge and expansive shrug, as if apologetically admitting the obvious truth that he had no power over the tides. Instead, he offered us a bed for the night.

We looked doubtfully, first at the newcomer and then at the closing hordes, a few of whom were now trying to clamber up Salamander's hull. Yorkie seemed to read our minds.

He spoke gently. "If they're going to steal from you, there isn't a lot you can do about it whether you stay on board or not."

We looked yet again at our stricken vessel, her hull listing gently to one side. I didn't fancy the idea of the children sleeping on board, in case Salamander rolled onto her side during the night. Nor did I fancy the idea of being invaded by marauding Portuguese looters.

With a sickening sense of foreboding, we nodded and thanked Yorkie both for his advice and his offer of lodgings. George and I climbed back on board to unload a few essentials. Without much enthusiasm, we ushered a few trespassers off the deck before pushing some supplies into a canvas bag. George lowered it over the side to Yorkie.

Once back on the beach, I took a final glance up at Salamander's oddly still and lifeless hull. She had proved herself to be wilful and downright bloody minded at times. All the same, it didn't seem fair to leave her now. She seemed so helpless and... well, so... sad !

Dismissing my thoughts as the rantings of exhaustion, I turned, leaving Salamander to the mercies of the locals and joined the forlorn crocodile of refugees following Yorkie up the beach. I carried a supermarket carrier bag in which I had hastily collected toothpaste, toothbrushes and a change of clothes for me, George and the girls. George had the canvas bag slung over his shoulder in which, I had no doubt, there would be a bottle or two. Zoe had a haversack on her back and the girls, of course, clutched a teddy bear each. All of life's essentials for our first night as castaways.

Yorkie led us towards a line of trees which gradually turned into a thick wood. We picked our way between into the darkness, the shadows becoming denser beneath the canopy of branches. Suddenly, the deep blue sky reappeared and, in a clearing scattered with the debris of many years basic living, stood a small, whitewashed stone shed. Our guide opened the unpainted timber door and we filed in, grateful at least for the shelter it offered.

A rose cheeked woman in her late thirties was immediately introduced to us as Yorkie's wife. She greeted us with no sign of surprise and a broad smile as if familiar neighbours had just called in for a cup of coffee and a gossip.

It was around 11 o'clock by now and our energies were almost spent. We had no strength to argue as they offered us the only two beds in their small home. The little protest we made was quickly waved aside as he and his wife smiled reassuringly and left the room. Yorkie was sure the new day would bring new ideas. George nodded optimistically.

"It'll be all right." He put his arm round me as the door closed with a rattle as a heavy metal latch fell into place. "You'll see."

We sat on the low timber bed and took stock of our new surroundings. Though dimly lit, it would have been difficult not to notice that the whitewashed walls were decorated almost entirely with dead animals and firearms. Shotguns, pistols and rifles of every description hung everywhere. A pair of old flintlock pistols of the sort Dick Turpin used to hold up mail coaches sat on rusty nails hammered roughly into the stone lintel over the fireplace. Above them, a stag's head poked out of the wall and eyed us curiously.

A few feet from him, in an alcove next to the chimney breast, a cowboy's revolver sat in a glass case just above a shelf where a weasel, standing on its hind legs, glared with lifeless glass eyes towards the front door.

Next to the window, a powerful hunting rifle, complete with telescopic sight, leaned casually into the corner. Next to it, apparently discarded just as easily, a double barrelled shotgun. Above the window, an ancient musket, five feet long, stretched the length of the curtain pole. I have never liked guns, despite being a country girl at heart. I felt a cold shiver moving between my shoulder blades and shuddered involuntarily.

My father had once taken me out shooting with a farmer friend of his. Despite being lectured on the need to keep vermin down and protect livestock, I failed to appreciate his shooting of two rabbits and a hare that morning. When the farmer had handed me the rifle and pointed to another rabbit at the far end of the field, I glared at him, dropped the weapon at his feet and shouted loudly enough to scare to unwitting creature away. I had stormed off while the farmer watched, totally bemused. Although father privately sympathised with me, his friendship with the farmer was never quite the same again.

Yorkie was apparently another follower of field sports but that didn't alter my natural sense of unease in the midst of his armoury. I swallowed hard. Perhaps, I suggested, he earned his living by hunting.

"Or gun running," sniffed George. "How many guns does it take to shoot a deer ?" This was not the sort of reassurance I wanted to hear. "On the other hand," he mused, climbing into bed, "perhaps he's a professional hit man."

I chastised him for frightening the children. In truth, they were far less concerned than I was. I pulled the rough blankets up to my chin and shuddered quietly.

"Don't worry." Said George. "If he is a hit man, he can't be a very good shot. Not if he's living like this."

As we drifted off, our curiosity and depression temporarily exhausted, Zoe let out a deep sigh. "It's all experience," she murmured. "Part of life's rich tapestry of dreams." She closed her eyes. "I'm going to have a Salamander dream."

"That's very deep." I said, yawning. "Is it something some ancient philosopher once said ?"

"Yup." She smiled in the darkness, remembering a long gone bedroom concert. "Charles Aznavour. He has an L.P called 'Tapestry of Dreams'."

"Don't think I've heard that one. Is he any good ?"

Zoe sniffed. "Nah. He's far too old for me. I only bought it for my mum. She thinks his French accent is sexy."

Despite our misgivings and guilty knowledge that our host and his long suffering wife were enduring a far less comfortable night on the floor of their shed, we slept soundly. Presumably they had a machine gun or two for comfort.

The following morning we headed back to the beach as early as we reasonably could without appearing ungrateful. Yorkie's wife had insisted on seating us round her table while she made us a large pot of coffee and hearty breakfast, even though we pleaded that we should take full advantage of all the daylight we could.

A throng of villagers arrived within minutes. Perhaps they had been there all night, watching from the shadows of the trees. A few policemen had now joined them and, seeing our apprehension, began to make some show of ushering the crowds back from the boat.

One of the officers took a step forward and saluted, bowing slightly. He wished us a good morning more, I felt, to show off his English than out of sincerity. He and his colleagues, were, he informed us, from Espinho, the nearest town. He waved vaguely first towards the other officers and then at the southern end of the beach. They were here to protect our possessions. If there was any other service they could render, we only had to ask.

George brightened immediately. He thanked him and asked whether a tug could be arranged to pull Salamander off the beach.

"Ah," sighed the officer, smiling kindly, "this you will have to arrange yourself."

We spent the next twelve hours ferrying our gear off Salamander and lining it up on the beach. In the meantime the policemen walked sagely up and down, surveying the booty with quietly growing interest. They wrote occasional notes in their notebooks, but made little attempt to stop the inquisitive locals from picking over the growing piles of salvage. We wondered which of our possessions in particular they intended to protect.

Before long we realised that, despite one of us continually standing sentry, for every four boxes of food or provisions we brought ashore, at least one disappeared. Odd pieces of equipment, particularly the more portable bits, also mysteriously vanished. Even barrels of marine fuel managed to walk off the beach when our backs were turned.

On each occasion we mentioned to any of the policemen that something else had gone missing, they shrugged happily and shook their heads. They could not explain, let alone prevent, things they had not seen. These acts of piracy they deemed unworthy of reporting in their notebooks.

On this first full day in Espinho we discovered how fast news can travel in a small town. An unusually smart car pulled up at the end of the track leading onto the beach, from which an equally smart young man emerged. He strode purposely across the sand and through the crowd that now seemed to have taken up permanent residence around us.

Stepping clear of the human cordon, he stuck out his hand and introduced himself. This was John; like Yorkie, an English ex-patriot who, we were to learn, had settled in the area and married a local Portuguese girl. He had heard that an English family had been marooned and thought we might like a hand. We nodded in unison. He looked at Salamander's hull and admitted he didn't know a lot about boats. But, he added brightly, he knew plenty of people who did.

He smiled broadly. "Apart from me, everybody in Espinho knows about boats. There isn't a great deal else they need to know about."

George scanned the crowd doubtfully. If this were true, they had been singularly reticent about their expertise.

The first thing we had to do, he went on, wass to find somewhere to stay. "I learned that years ago from reading

Robinson Crusoe." He chuckled at his own joke. "Come on then." He scooped up a box of clothes. "Let's get you sorted."

We followed him, somewhat dazed by the rapid passage of events, up the sand. He filled the boot of his car with our gear and we all piled in, still quite unsure of where we were going. The girls, sitting on our laps in the back, watched fascinated as we entered the little town. It's hard to remember the intense excitement that, as young children, we must have all once felt when making new discoveries.

John and Fernander, his wife, unhesitatingly offered us their spare room. Their kindness, shown for complete strangers, left me totally lost for words. Speechlessness was a rare experience for me, and one that George keeps telling me I should practice more !

That afternoon we set about our salvage work with a vengeance. Our rough calculations suggested that if we could sell enough non-essential equipment and possessions, and despite Yorkie's pessimistic predictions, we might be able to raise sufficient funds to hire a tug and tow Salamander out to sea. With any luck we would have enough provisions and fuel left to get to Gibraltar. There, we might be able to find work and gather enough money to carry us on to our next step.

In the meantime we had a few hundred pounds left which we offered to Zoe to buy an air ticket home. She flatly refused. She had come this far, she said, and was in no mood to leave the job half done. I was so proud of her determination and quite ashamed of myself for having ever doubted that a go-go dancer could make a suitable sailor.

We were often to reflect that of all our crew it had been Zoe that George and I had been most concerned about. George has always said my judgement of people's character starts from a point of either totally trusting or mistrusting them – and is therefore usually proved wrong. Most people, he says, tell the truth some of the time, white lies for most of the time and downright howlers for the few minutes that remain each day. The trick, then, is to identify who does which, in what proportion and when. It is this trick that, I openly confess, I have never mastered. George, on the other hand, normally gets it about right. On this occasion, we were both happy to admit we had been wrong.

On our third day in Espinho, 10th September, John and Fernander took me, Zoe and the girls a few miles to the larger town of Porto. Here, they claimed, was the largest market in Portugal. After wandering up and down the rows of stalls for a few hours, it seemed to me that their boast was probably justified. The town was vast after the narrow streets of Espinho. The market place alone seemed bigger than the entire village. It seemed possible to buy absolutely anything and at every corner a bedraggled beggar would sit cross legged, his hand outstretched for a few Escudos.

It was a humbling experience and made me realise how fortunate we were. We still had each other and the apparently unconditional friendship of Yorkie, his wife, John and Fernander more than made up for our encounters with the likes of Captain Dan, the Dorey skipper, Lucifer and the police officers of Brest and Muros.

The market visit made a welcome break from working on the boat, although we all knew we should spend as little as possible on non-essentials. As yet, we didn't know how much it was going to cost to get afloat again. Right from the start, our funds had been limited.

We soon became quite accustomed to visitors as we laboured up and down the beach, portering boxes to John's car. While the attending police officers seldom bothered us, neither did they pay any attention to the comings and goings of the locals (particularly their goings). Although we tried not to leave anything of any great value unattended, the area seemed to thrive on scavenging. The same had been true along the coasts of England and the Channel Islands a century ago and the tradition, having survived here for so long, wasn't going to change for our benefit.

As islanders ourselves, we well understood the way that coastal people have to make a living out by wrecking. Even so, it was unusual for salvagers to be at work while the legitimate owners were still so close by.

There was one visitor to the beach, other than John, who stood out from the rest. He seemed, unusually, to be there for a legitimate purpose rather than as a sightseer or opportunist thief. Certainly, if he was a thief, he was too well dressed to be anything but a very good one. In his late thirties and self assured, he had the air of one who would be at ease in any social situation.

He shook us each warmly by the hand, smiling and waving away George's apologies for his habitual layer of oil. He introduced himself as Jorge and produced a small business card. Clearly impressed, George wiped his hands before accepting it. Jorge translated from the Portuguese, announcing that he was a reporter for the local newspaper. And we, he cheerfully informed us, were local celebrities.

"It is the same the world over." He beamed broadly. "The public loves to read about celebrities – especially local ones." He was sure his readers were no different.

"They would be interested to know your story." He smiled reassuringly and nodded as if to confirm our agreement, although we hadn't spoken a word. He pulled a small pad of paper and an elegant silver pen from his pocket. He smiled again, clicking the button at the end of the pen with an exaggerated flick of his wrist. Rapidly he scribbled some notes. While we were answering his questions another man appeared, the gathered crowd parting to allow him through. Younger, slighter in build, he was struggling through the soft sand and clutching a small but apparently heavy aluminium case.

The second man nodded briefly to Jorge before looking about, apparently for somewhere to put his case. He decided on the flat top of an oil barrel, using it as a table to set the case down before opening it. From within, he produced an elaborate collection of camera parts which, with great ceremony he proceeded to piece together.

A few of the children had gathered closer to watch and, after smiling benevolently, his camera now complete, he gently moved them aside.

Jorge asked us, rather pointlessly, if we minded having our photograph taken for the newspaper. The photographer was already going about his work, moving enthusiastically around, squatting down to catch our portraits with Salamander's hull looming as a vast backdrop behind us. Next, he ushered Tania and Kim towards us before jumping up onto one of the barrels, wobbling perilously, and taking a wide shot of the five of us, surrounded by our scattered belongings.

Next, he was dancing lithely between the rocks, clattering off photographs of our sad piles of possessions, posing Tania, Kim and then Zoe around them. Zoe seemed to be getting the lion's share of his attention. He posed her first sitting, then leaning on a rock, then an oil drum, first looking one way, then the other. Eagerly, he placed her hand on her hip, then shading her eyes, gazing out to sea. She smiled politely, complying, now with one hand behind her head, face up to the clouds, eyes shut, then head down in melancholy muse towards the sand.

Jorge watched, an apologetic smile across his face. He closed his notebook and shrugged. "He enjoys his work." He thanked us for our time and asked if he might speak with us again if his editor decided to print a follow-up story.

He patted the photographer on the shoulder, beckoning. Reluctantly, the camera was packed away. The photographer shook Zoe by the hand, lingering a fraction longer than was necessary. He grinned sheepishly at us before following Jorge through the sand.

So began our friendship with Journalist Jorge.

There was nobody worth knowing in Espinho or Porto, we soon learned, who Jorge didn't know. And if he didn't know them, he knew someone who did. Having written his piece about us for the newspaper, he now devoted every spare moment to guiding us round the area, introducing us to boat owners who might be able to help us get back to sea or, failing that, might buy some of our fittings to provide us with funds.

With Journalist Jorge's help we at least began to understand the nature of the task now facing us. Even so, our progress in clearing Salamander was painfully slow. The local police had been working invisibly behind the scenes, making out reports to a broad selection of Government Ministries. As a result a lengthening string of officials now seemed to have become involved, all apparently concerned with a different aspect of our dilemma. Each one, clutching a briefcase stuffed with forms and regulations, required some sort of information or list from us. Our passport numbers, our last port of call, the date of our arrival, the proposed date of our departure, the nature of our cargo, the value of our possessions, Salamander's value, her tonnage, capacity and port of registration. All had to be recorded, apparently in triplicate, as we were asked each question at least three times, the replies to be entered in a Ministry file somewhere.

Another anonymous official, one of a lengthening queue, wished to know the precise purpose of our visit to Espinho and the duration of our stay. Were we aware, he politely asked, that we had landed illegally? He leafed through yet another dossier about us, compiled by yet another Government department. It appeared, he looked up over his half framed spectacles, that we had failed to obtain the necessary permission to visit Portugal. We had no visas permitting us to work here.

George smiled confidently. We had done no work. The official flipped over the next page in his file.

"Neither have you been issued with visas to visit as tourists." He delivered another piercing gaze over the spectacles. "This," he said seriously, "is an offence against the Republic of Portugal for which a heavy fine can be imposed." He looked us up and down. If we were unable to pay, our possessions could be confiscated. "Extradition", he intoned with deliberate menace, "is possible should you prove uncooperative."

We nodded. This last option seemed to be the most helpful we had heard so far. George asked how we might apply. I giggled, checking myself by coughing into my hand. The official gazed at us, devoid of emotion.

"I do not understand, Mr Russell."

George looked downcast. He turned to me. "I don't think he's got the right forms with him." I giggled again, now beyond disguise. The official left, convinced he was dealing with a family of lunatics.

Jorge now took us through the winding labyrinth of Porto's Government offices. He acted as taxi driver, interpreter and advocate. Where red tape blocked our way, Jorge seemed to know how to cut it. When necessary, he negotiated on our behalf to get whatever permission or concession we needed to proceed.

Jorge's status was swiftly elevated, in our estimation at least, to greater and dizzier heights and it wasn't long before he had earned the title of Saint Jorge.

CHAPTER FIVE

Settling and Salvaging

Had I been asked a few months earlier, I would have been quite clear that I would never have considered spending a Saturday cleaning a grave, least of all a Portuguese one belonging to someone I had never had the privilege of meeting. In Espinho, however, such activities were just as likely to become part of our strange routine as cooking a meal or washing our laundry. Even this mundane practice, we would discover, was to take a different twist in Espinho.

Fernander told me, one Friday evening, that she would shortly be going to visit her grandmother. It was after several minutes of discussion on the virtues of a grandparent's influence on young children and the joys of family unity, that it dawned on me that the grandmother in question had been dead for several years.

Fernander nodded cheerfully. She was buried at the village cemetery and out of courtesy I agreed that making regular family visits seemed a nice tradition. Before I knew what I had triggered off, Zoe, the children and I had been recruited. By 7.30 the following morning we were being marched through the centre of the village carrying brushes, buckets and cleaning cloths.

As in most Catholic countries, cremations are virtually unheard of in Portugal. Instead, coffins are interred in specially constructed caverns in the cemetery walls. In Espinho, as in most cemeteries in southern Europe, these were adorned with photographs of the deceased along with freshly cut flowers, regularly refreshed, and candles kept burning inside small decorative lanterns.

Each sarcophagus was carefully engraved with the details of its occupant. In some cases entire families occupied a family tomb, their surname displayed in gold lettering above large iron lattice doors. The entire area seemed to be built in white marble, although an occasional splash of mottled grey or pink indicated the presence of a more avant garde, or perhaps just wealthier, family.

It could be partly because the families of this little town tended to remain for several generations in the same area, if not the same street or even the same house that they were able to tend so diligently to their ancestors. Whatever the reason, their devotion was clear. The candles didn't expire. The flowers didn't wilt. The memories didn't fade.

Fernander solemnly introduced us all to her grandmother and we, somewhat uncomfortably at first, set about cleaning the white memorial stone while she replaced the flowers and the fat red church candle. Its wick flickering yellow once more inside a glass walled lantern, she sat down quietly on a stone bench and gazed at our handiwork.

My cleaning duties complete and sensing Fernander's need to be alone for a while, I took a few moments to wander around in silence between the memorials. I was immediately uplifted and humbled by the sheer neatness of the place.

Had this been an Anglican churchyard I would have probably been only too keen to leave. I have always had a sense of foreboding about such places, especially as the English variety I had been used to were, in my experience, usually over-grown with ivy and brambles. Here, there was something different which made me want to linger and quietly enjoy rather than to retreat.

At first, I found it difficult to identify exactly what that strange ingredient was. There were the flowers, decorations, engravings and memorial sculptures. They all contributed, it's true, but there was something else. For several minutes I couldn't put my finger on it. There was nothing tangible which gave the little cemetery its unexpected charm, but rather something that was completely lacking. It dawned on me that the area enclosed within the high stone walls was swathed in a protective, sun-lit blanket of silence. However hard I strained to hear the sounds of the world outside, I could hear absolutely nothing.

This wonderful tranquillity, rather like the bay at Muros on that calm day, had turned this little corner of Espinho into a haven.

We walked back to John and Fernander's home in silence, unsure whether we were subconsciously doing so as a sign of respect, or simply because we couldn't bring ourselves to shatter the calm. I certainly didn't voice my thoughts on how our churchyards would compare or how our own family graves were cared for.

As if to provide a total contrast, it was Tania's fifth birthday a few days later. We took her to the local swimming pool. It was part of a wonderful municipal recreation centre, complete with a bar, cafe and restaurant. It had swings, a see-saw and slides into the pool. A small clay sports pitch was marked out for football, basketball and volleyball matches with a separate, larger, area given pride of place for the local hockey team. For such a small town, Espinho's civic authorities seemed to go out of their way to provide a healthy variety of activities for their citizens.

Here, between splashing, shrieking, leaping, sliding and diving, and in as many riotous ways as she could, Tania swam for the first time. Had it not all been so exciting, she would have been thoroughly exhausted by the time we returned to John and Fernander's house.

In our absence, they had laid on a party for her, inviting all their neighbours and local children. It was the most wonderful children's party I had ever been to with large quantities of wine, port and champagne, along with five truly gorgeous home baked cakes.

Zoe and I wondered what the Portuguese would have made of our rather mundane children's party fayre. Somehow, we thought, red jelly and jam sandwiches wouldn't quite have stood up to comparison.

We had thoroughly enjoyed our day out. It gave us pause for reflection, not for the first or the last time, at the extent of Espinho's hospitality. Our little Channel Island has a long tradition of offering a welcome to travellers, whatever fortune or misfortune takes them there. Whether or not a Portuguese boat owner, stranded on the beach outside St.Peter Port, would have received the same open handed generosity is, however, open to speculation.

As time progressed, we came to the realisation that we wouldn't, for several reasons, be able to keep many of our possessions. Those things that we had left aboard Salamander were steadily being decimated by looters and we were fighting a losing battle to rescue those they had so far left behind. Squeezed into the spare bedroom in John and Fernander's little home, and already feeling guilty that we were occupying so much of their limited space, there was barely room to hang the clothes we wore each day. Our small reserve of cash was also fast draining away.

We set September 25th aside exclusively to sort through all the possessions we had brought off the boat. We placed them in four piles; the first for things we would give away. The second was to be given specifically to the local orphanage. The third pile was for bits and pieces we would try to sell in order to increase our 'moving on' fund. The fourth and smallest pile was for those things we intended to keep.

The orphanage pile grew steadily. Made up entirely of Kim and Tania's clothes and toys, I was amazed at how calmly they accepted it – admittedly sweetened by the promise of a new bike each at some unspecified future date. Child psychologists will be howling with indignation, but these desperate times called for desperate measures; bribery and dodgy dealing included.

On the subject of corruption, we were given warnings about the contents of that third little pile that we intended to sell. Secrecy, apparently, was crucial. Under Portuguese law we were obliged to hand over to the Government all proceeds of anything we sold. They would then, apparently, after due deliberation, apply their own estimates of how much they believed our goods had actually been worth (not necessarily the amount we had received for them) and thereafter, how much tax they would charge.

We were confidently informed by several well meaning officials that there would, at some point, be a pronouncement on how much money we would be allowed to have back. Thereafter, we could apply to the appropriate office for permission to claim it.

Each part of this process, we were warned by those who knew the system, could take months – even with our red tape cutting Journalist (Saint) Jorge at the helm !

It was widely believed that such governmental delays were dragged out quite deliberately. Claimants who left the country, or even the municipality, before the process was complete automatically lost all rights to what was left of their cash. Listening to John and Jorge patiently explaining these local customs made us almost homesick for the disinterest the Guernsey authorities show for most forms of taxation.

We asked what our chances were of hiding from the civil servants and quietly bartering our goods away at the local market. Jorge's newspaper article and the inevitable attention we had drawn to ourselves in the little village, however, had made discretion completely impossible.

We were faced with little alternative but to press on, salvage all we could, declare whatever we had to and compensate ourselves for as much of our loss as possible.

We still had the spark of a notion at the back of our minds. If the propeller could be freed from the sand and removed, with a high tide and a bit of luck (which we reckoned we were owed) we would be able to pull Salamander off the beach. We would, of course, need a powerful tug but anything non essential that we could take off her would reduce her weight.

There was therefore a double incentive to our salvage operation of raising funds and, in a manner of speaking, raising Salamander. George spent days studying the waterline along the beach. He reckoned that, with a low tide and a calm day, we could dig a large enough hole round the propeller to remove it before the tide returned and filled it up with sand again.

At about this time Jorge brought us the news that one of the many local Government officials who had taken such an interest in us was getting upset that Salamander was cluttering up his beach. We were more intrigued than worried, wondering what the unnamed bureaucrat was going to suggest we do about it.

Saint Jorge smiled and assured us this was good news. The Portuguese Navy, he said, were being called in.

"God," I muttered, clutching George with one hand and Saint Jorge with the other. "They're going to blast her off the beach !"

A mental picture formed in Jorge's mind and his smile broadened as he wondered how best to transcribe the forthcoming manoeuvres for his next newspaper article.

"It could make a very funny cartoon." he thought aloud.

George almost exploded. "Funny ? It wouldn't be bloody funny at all ! It would be bloody serious !" He saw Jorge's shy smile and hands raised in mock surrender. Chastened, George quickly tried to join in the joke. "All that matchwood all over the beach. Not funny at all. Just think of the litter."

Jorge waggled his finger, tutting at our disparaging opinion of his nation's armed forces. "Portugal" he promised us, sticking out his chest, "has the finest navy in the World." He paused for a moment's reflection. "Maybe not the biggest." He nodded conclusively. "They will free Salamander from her beach. You will see."

A hazy recollection drifted into my consciousness. Many years before, sitting in a classroom, I had been vaguely aware of one of my unfortunate teachers trying to shove some history into me. Her hope had been entirely in vain, although I was sure she had said something about the Portuguese Discovery Boats. Hadn't Vasco da Gama (or was it Marco Polo?) or someone like that come from Portugal? Either way, the Portuguese had done an awful lot of discovering, or pirating at least, in places like China or South America (or somewhere a long way away, anyhow). If they could do that all those centuries ago, surely they could pull a little boat off one of their own beaches.

I put this hypothesis to George who, it has to be said, didn't seem quite as reassured as I was. Nevertheless, he managed a slight nod and a quiet "It'll be all right" before lapsing into a long and thoughtful silence.

Jorge did his best to learn the Navy's plans, without success, and we were left biting our nails until the appointed day to discover Salamander's fate. In the meantime, we assembled each day at low tide to tunnel under the propeller and remove it. The plan failed only because the retaining bolt was rusted solid.

Come the great day, we assembled on the beach to await the arrival of the mighty Portuguese fleet. A variety of miscellaneous officials, easily identified by briefcases and clip boards, muttered assurances to each other about tides and naval timetables. Meanwhile, the hours passed tediously by.

John and Fernander strolled up and down the beach, their arms round each other while Jorge relaxed, spread out on a deckchair he had brought for the occasion. He apparently understood the vagaries of his nation's Navy better than the civil servants.

The photographer had reappeared with his aluminium case and had, for the two hours since his discovery that Zoe wasn't willing to be photographed again, been anxiously glancing at his watch.

Occasionally Jorge glanced up to reassure him and, for the rest of the time, read casually through his copy of that morning's newspaper. His attention seemed to have been captured by a single page. Every so often he would flip the paper noisily and utter a brief exclamation or clench his fist, punching the air briefly like a boxer playing to the cameras at a pre-match press conference.

Finally, I nudged John and asked him what he was reading. John sauntered over and glanced briefly over Jorge's shoulder.

"It is an article about predicted water shortages."

I glanced at Jorge. "I didn't realise it was such an emotive subject."

"It isn't." John shrugged. "It's just that he wrote it."

Jorge suddenly became aware that he was the centre of our attention and closed his newspaper. "O.K," he said. "But it's a good piece. I really get to the *heart* of it." He clenched his fist again for emphasis.

At that moment, and to everybody's excitement, Zoe pointed along the line of the beach and shouted. Following the line of her finger, we saw a grey tug appearing from a distant headland. George raised his war-surplus binoculars and, having studied the vessel more closely, announced she had a naval style serial number on her prow. She also had a military pennant fluttering in the breeze at her stern. As the minutes ticked by, she followed a slow line parallel to the shore until she had positioned herself adjacent to where we stood. About a mile out to sea, the tug had now slowed and appeared to be turning to shore. I asked George, whose binoculars were still studying its progress, what he thought it was doing. Wordlessly, he shook his head.

Finally, the binoculars lowered and, shrugging, he admitted there were only two things he could be sure of; the tug belonged to the Portuguese Navy. And it was doing very little.

Several of the officials glanced at their watches and made notes on their clip boards. The photographer started the ritual of unpacking his case and bolting bits of his camera together.

Gradually, the tug closed in on us before drifting to a halt. For about half an hour, George and the tug motionlessly observed one another. Finally, he announced, "she's moving."

We all saw it then; the tiny bow wave and thin trail of smoke from the exhaust. But instead of coming towards us, the tug seemed to be turning. The officials murmured to each other, checked their watches again and made further notes. Within forty minutes the vessel had manoeuvred through a wide arc and disappeared once again behind the headland. Maybe it had gone to get some extra equipment ? More crew perhaps ? Another tug ?

Jorge now became more animated, rising from his deck chair for the first time since the proceedings had begun. He pinpointed the key members of the beach party and asked for explanations. It was clear from the broad shrugs and head shaking that the officials didn't have an answer either.

Our speculation was interrupted by the arrival of a high pitched and extremely noisy moped. It slewed to a halt and unsteadily sank into the sand beneath its rider; a skinny lad wearing a short sleeved shirt beneath an outsized cap. This apparently denoted that he belonged to one of the officials present, for he quickly singled out one of the briefcase carriers and handed over a bit of paper.

The recipient read the paper twice before slapping it angrily with the back of his hand. He passed it to the official standing next to him who, in turn, read it, slapped it and handed it along the line. The original recipient of the note shouted at the unfortunate moped rider who seemed to shrivel even further beneath his government issue cap.

His attention turned to the other briefcases and clip boards and the minuscule messenger beat an opportunistic retreat, leaping on his machine, thrusting down on one of the pedals and showering us all in sand in his haste to escape.

Jorge delivered the news, though we barely needed a translation. The captain of the tug had judged Salamander to be too large for his vessel to cope with and, more significantly, too far up the beach even though it was now high tide. Unwilling to expend further time or effort – or risk the humiliation of failure – he had decided to return to port without attempting a rescue.

Mildly disappointed that their afternoon's entertainment had been curtailed, the locals sauntered back to the village. The photographer muttered a dark oath at Jorge, tapped his watch furiously, and packed his camera away again. Jorge simply folded his newspaper, tucking it and his deckchair under his arm and plodded quietly back to his car.

George, Zoe, the girls and I decided to go for a walk along the beach. For the time being there didn't seem to be anything else worth doing.

George was curiously silent as the girls chased and chattered about us and Zoe seemed engrossed in a pebble Tania had given her for safe keeping. I threaded my arm through George's, his hand rammed deep in his trouser pocket. We didn't need to speak to understand what we were both thinking.

We paused at the foot of a low sea cliff and sat on the rocks while the girls burned off some more energy. Only now did we speak. By the time we resumed our walk we had come to the conclusion, finally and with great sadness, that Salamander could not be saved. She would have to be broken up for salvage.

It was a decision we had been dreading and one which we had hoped would never have to be made. We were even quieter during our walk home. For George, never one to prattle even at his most animated, this meant a journey in total silence.

The lull in activity gave us a chance to reflect. In a few days time John and Fernander were to travel to England for one of several regular holidays they took each year with his family. Had we been beached a few weeks earlier or later during a time when they were away, we would quite probably have been homeless. They were perfectly happy to let us stay in their home while they were in England and offered to post any letters for us while they were there.

I suddenly realised I had not written to my mother since our impromptu arrival in Espinho and was immediately driven by conscience to pick up a pen and write her a postcard. Hence it was that almost a week later my mother received a Portuguese postcard postmarked Kidderminster, Worcs.

'Dear Mum', I wrote, wondering how I was going to break the news. 'Having a real adventure – landed in Portugal near Porto – 12 miles away ...' I read over what I had just written. So far, so good. Nothing to worry her yet. '...*Will have to sell the boat if possible'.* I paused. Well, that might be a little bit unexpected. I'd better just explain. *'... Managed to ground her. We are all safe and happy living with the Portuguese'* O.K, so that may sound a bit like a Victorian explorer writing home from Central Africa, "living with the natives". At least it got the bad news out of the way quickly enough and made it sound like it's all turned out fine. Better continue on the same note. *'... Met a great chap called John who will take this card to London to post to you for quickness. We will try to get to Gibraltar for winter and be happy to return home in spring having made a fortune'.* Very positive. A bit more along those lines just to make sure. *'...Been busy trying to remove everything from ship. The children are making friends everywhere and having a whale of a time. Will send a forwarding address as soon as possible. We will be here approximately three weeks. It makes a change from the 9 to 5 !'*

I re-read the card half a dozen times, searching for anything that might worry her. Eventually, having tested it out on George and Zoe and agreeing it hit the right cheery note, I handed it over to our personal courier.

The following two days were spent 'Salamandering' as we now called it. Either knee or elbow deep in varying parts of her bowels, we removed those parts of her that we could man-handle (or should that be person-handle ?) and which might be saleable in and around a Portuguese fishing village.

By 8.30 pm of the following day we had removed half the batteries. They weighed over 60 lbs each, but lined up along the beach and dwarfed by the great hull standing over them, they looked like so many toy building blocks.

The following day we set about unbolting the generator. For George, particularly, this was the point of no return. Batteries could be replaced relatively easily. Without a generator, though, Salamander lost her heart. The radio and lights which had given us hospitality, even when her engine had refused to start, would never work again. From that moment, the air pressure she needed could no longer be produced and that ancient, stubborn, bloody minded engine wouldn't turn, let alone drum or roar for us again.

Adding to the pain and misery, George concluded that in order to get the generator out, he would have to cut a large hole in the solid timber decking. It seemed such a tragic waste to cut her up. Even the propeller, still deeply embedded in the sand, would have to be salvaged to help raise the cash we needed.

We had already failed to recover it once but George reckoned it was definitely worth another try. A ship's propeller is one of those wonderfully sculptured pieces of brass that is instantly saleable, if only as decoration for a bar or café – which is exactly what it was later used as.

We were cheering ourselves up, now, thinking of going on to the south of France. Whatever our destination, we had all agreed, our priority was to get there as soon as possible. We didn't fancy spending a winter in the area, having been warned that when the rains hit the west coast of Portugal, the entire region could easily be brought to a swampy standstill for weeks at a time.

Enthusiasm for pastures new mingled with an urgency to escape before the weather deteriorated. They overshadowed our sadness and pushed us on as we stripped out everything that could be unscrewed, unbolted or otherwise extracted.

Technical bric-a-brac like the compressor mask, regulator, compass and drive wheels were soon joined by more decorative bric-a-brac like brass port holes and fittings from the galley. We thought of the salvage sales at home and wondered how much we would have been able to raise had we been in Guernsey. Such 'Catch-22' thoughts were wholly pointless. We couldn't get home until we had sold our salvage, however low the local market prices were. Although we hadn't established how much local people would be prepared to pay, we were sure it would be a lot less than in the Channel Islands.

Our daily toils were interrupted periodically by generous efforts by our hosts to entertain us. A visit to the cinema to see a double feature which ran from 9.30 in the evening until the early hours of the morning seemed quite normal to John and Fernander, but totally exhausted us.

Being a Hollywood production, the film was in English, although the Portuguese sub-titles did little to enhance a tortuous tale of a woman who gave birth to a severely disabled child, only to learn it was all the fault of drugs she had been prescribed in pregnancy. The film concentrated on her battle with the way the media portrayed her and the legal battle between her, a small army of doctors and a giant pharmaceutical company. It wasn't the sort of film George and I would have chosen to see at home. At any other time, I doubt that I would have paid much heed to it. In my present state of mind, however, its turgid message reminded me of how profoundly lucky we had all been to walk onto Espinho's beach those few weeks before.

Between Salamandering sessions, our days dragged as we waited for decisions to be made by officials. It was in their gift to determine what, if anything, we could keep, what we could sell and what their Government intended to keep for itself. Neither had we yet heard what the authorities intended to do about our reckless crime spree. We had, after all, illegally crossed a foreign boundary (to wit, Espinho beach). We were illegally residing in a country outside the European Economic Community (to wit, Portugal). We had illegally imported diverse and sundry items into said country without paying duty (to wit, several boxes of tinned food and various items of clothing, much of which had been pilfered before it even crossed the foreshore. And, of course, a boat). We continued to use an illegal mooring, despite dire warnings of the consequences (we did rather question the use of the word mooring. We thought 'parking' might have been more appropriate). Finally, we had illegally deposited litter on a beach in the shape of said boat plus contents of same.

How, we wanted to know, could we be accused of three different offences, all for accidentally running Salamander onto the beach. For that one single act, we were being threatened with prosecution for illegally importing it, illegal mooring and fly-tipping !

Jorge explained with a shrug. One was the province of the Immigration Service, another the responsibility of the Excise Department and the third was down to the Provincial Council. They all wanted their pound of flesh.

While Saint Jorge explained to the third exasperated official in succession that none of our actions had been through choice, John, Fernander and a variety of their friends had the good sense to disappear for a three day trip to Lisbon prior to their flight to England. In their absence, we spent many hours waiting for our Saint to bring us news or instruct us in the completion of yet another government form.

Meanwhile, he continued to press home our argument (which he professed to agree with wholeheartedly) that most of our allegedly illegal goods had now been pilfered because of delays created by the tardy behaviour of the Government agencies involved. Pilfered, he added, by the very people who the exasperated bureaucrats claimed their taxes were going to help. And what had the police done about the thefts? Had they charged anyone with theft? Had they even investigated? Of course not. If no money had been paid for the goods, how could they incur any tax?

Jorge came from a well respected local family and his lucid and well argued interventions were, at least, given a polite hearing. Despite this, he confided that he doubted the officials would report his arguments too clearly to their superiors. He suspected he was merely being tolerated or, worse, humoured.

At the end of one such meeting we had heard a loud guffaw of laughter emitting from behind the office door we had just been ushered through. On another occasion the official could barely conceal his outrage that his Ministry's rules were being questioned by a bunch of illegal immigrants. They were, Jorge concluded, competing for brownie points against. The more revenue they could extract from errant foreigners, the greater their kudos. The official line was simply that they were following Government policy and enforcing the law.

Jorge determined to speak directly with their superiors. He set about arranging appointments with senior ministry officials and organising a trip to Lisbon. Meanwhile, we sat and awaited our fate.

In the closing days of September and before any of the Government departments had issued a reply to his requests, the mighty Portuguese administrative machine issued the product of its deliberations. Jorge tore open the buff coloured envelope as we stood uncomfortably waiting, like academically failing pupils awaiting their father's response to their school reports.

Jorge's expression gave nothing away as his eyes flickered along the lines. He cleared his throat and began to translate aloud as he went through the letter for a second time. It was from the mayor's office and represented the sum of several rulings made by various arms of the regional council. We were, by order of someone somewhere who was probably terribly senior and important, graciously given permission to sell Salamander or any part of her that could be salvaged. This was conditional on us signing an undertaking that we would fully disclose all monies received and immediately pay any taxes, duties and sundry other charges they might demand.

Jorge looked up in some resignation. They apparently intended to dream up a few more taxes to add to the bills already lined up for the coming weeks. On the bright side, though, we had at least received official permission to sell our salvage.

We were also given permission to stay in the country until our work clearing the beach had been completed.

The decisions, which Jorge said, despite everything, were a great step forward, caused us no little discomfort. We hadn't realised we needed permission to sell things anyway. We had been making attempts all along, albeit with little success, to sell everything that was no longer essential.

Jorge explained, as if we hadn't already worked it out for ourselves, that the Government had to give their permission, if only because they wanted their tax. And they had to allow us to stay in the country, as they clearly wouldn't be able to collect any tax from us after we had left.

"There is", he added unnecessarily, "always a price to pay." We worked out that if we managed to sell absolutely everything, after paying taxes at the rate Jorge thought we would be charged, we might be left with around £1,000.

Staring forlornly out of the window, George reflected with uncharacteristic melancholy that if they invented any new charges there wouldn't be any point in selling anything. We might just as well wait for a moonless night, grab all we could carry, and make a run for it.

Saint Jorge shrugged broadly and apologised at some length. It was the best settlement he had been able to get. "Of course, if you can wait longer I may be able to get a better deal..."

We shook our heads. He had spent many days of hard negotiation on our behalf to get this far and we couldn't ask him to waste any more time – nor take the chance that they might withdraw their offer altogether. Besides, Jorge's wife was expecting a baby, due any time now. He was also looking after his six year old daughter and trying to earn a living. We already felt guilty about taking him away from his family, so we thanked him profusely and assured him of our confidence in him. We were sure that he had already pulled as many strings and gained the best deal possible.

I was concerned that we should show our gratitude in some tangible way but Jorge flatly refused to accept any sort of reward. He assured us he had enjoyed the experience.

"I like people" he promised us, "and helping people is my way of life." He grinned impishly. "Especially if it means having a fight with the Government."

George and I began working out how many hours of hard graft it was now going to take to earn the sum we needed and that the Government was prepared to let us keep. About a third of the way through our calculation it became too depressing and we gave up. Instead, we consoled ourselves that it was better than a poke in the eye with the proverbial hot stick. After all, if Salamander had struck a rock and sunk, we wouldn't have had anything at all.

Despite George's suggestion of doing a bunk, we had no real intention of running out on our obligations, especially after we had been shown such kindness by John, Fernander and Saint Jorge. We couldn't bear the thought of leaving anything to rot on the beach that could and should be removed. Apart from any moral obligations, to do so would have made us guilty of real crimes. Whether the offences we were being accused of were genuine or not, at least we could stand on our small clump of moral high ground and say we had broken the law inadvertently and nobody had suffered unduly as a result. If we deliberately broke the law now, we imagined the Portuguese statute book would have been well and truly hurled at our retreating backs. Equally, Interpol might be despatched to track us down and chuck us in the nearest jail until we stumped up an even more exorbitant fine.

We resolved that, by staying and doing what we could, however unsuccessfully, we could at least plead in mitigation that we had done everything possible to clear the beach and pay our dues.

The completion, for the time being at least, of Jorge's work on our behalf, along with John and Fernander's brief absence gave us time for reflection on our domestic arrangements. We had now spent three weeks living in one room and although we were enormously grateful to our host and hostess, we felt there was a limit to the time we could either impose ourselves or expect Zoe to live with no privacy.

After one of the regular visits that Zoe and I made with the girls to the playground in the local park, we called at a camp site to make enquiries over alternative accommodation.

We thought a two bedroom tent would suit us and had often seen the sign outside the site advertising their facilities. No sooner had we walked through the broad gates and into the office than we were told it was due to close the following day and wouldn't re-open until next spring.

The owner must have seen our disappointment and, like everyone else in Espinho, knew all about our misadventures.

He gave a reassuring nod. We could stay, anyway. And as the site would be closed, we wouldn't have to pay any rent.

The site owner smiled, waving away our thanks. "There is one thing. You must know the winter rains are soon to start ?"

We nodded. We knew all about the rains. They had been the major topic of conversation around Espinho's cafes for the last couple of weeks. We backed out of the office, thanking him as we went before he could change his mind.

"You know what I think ?" I asked Zoe, rather pointlessly, as we walked back towards the village. She didn't, so I told her. "I reckon the well-to-do of Espinho are competing for a newly invented 'Generosity to Castaways' prize."

"There is just one problem." It wasn't like Zoe to find problems. "Where are we going to find a tent ?"

George and I had talked about that the night before. We remembered seeing a camping shop in Porto and the next time we had an opportunity to visit the town would price everything we needed.

1st October is George and my wedding anniversary. Normally, we might have taken ourselves off to a restaurant or visited our families. This year, of course, we had a rather different itinerary. We plodded down to the beach, George with his tool box, me and Zoe with Kim and Tania.

While we worked on the boat, watching the girls playing by the edge of the water, we were only mildly concerned by a family group who seemed to have struck up a conversation with them.

As they dispersed, we noticed something strange about the girls. They remained huddled together, peering down at the sand between them. It was unlike them to remain quite so inanimate for so long and Zoe was despatched to investigate.

She returned a few minutes later, the girls tripping along at her side. Wrapped in her cupped hands she carried a small brown bundle which she held out for my inspection. The visiting family, with all good intentions, had given the girls a puppy.

Of indeterminate breed, it had large liquid brown eyes and soft, ragged ears. Almost immediately, as I reached out to stroke it, it began licking my hand, laying one tiny paw across my thumb and, struggling as it spread across Zoe's palm, wagged its tail.

This, of course, to use an over exercised cliché, is one of every parent's long list of nightmares. It isn't that I don't like dogs. For most of our married life, George and I have shared our home with at least one dog. On this occasion, however, the parental foot had to be put down. This was not the right time to be adopting pets of any description.

I hurriedly went in search of the family, my heart pounding more rapidly than it had since the night we had run aground. Clambering over a large rock and rounding a headland into the next bay, I spotted them at the far end of the beach, heading into the village. Chasing and shouting until they stopped, I thanked them as graciously as I could, bearing in mind I was panting like a marathon runner, and apologetically returned the small ball of fluff to them. It, and they, gazed back at me with a mixture of wide eyed confusion and sadness. I swallowed hard, thanked them again and left before my sentimental side got the better of me.

September having turned relentlessly into October, Salamandering was becoming increasingly arduous. Most of the smaller, lighter pieces of equipment had already been recovered and, as the weather closed in, working conditions became more uncomfortable. The darker evenings slowed our progress and George, having asked where he might find some lifting gear, now approached a local garage that had a well equipped workshop. With John's assistance, he opened negotiations with the owner.

Finally it was agreed that, in exchange for his help and the use of a large lifting rig to remove the generator, compressor and mast, we would let him keep what was left of Salamander and all her remaining salvage. A month earlier, the very thought of brokering such a deal would have been preposterous. The passage of time and deteriorating weather, however, had quickly put our priorities in perspective.

The wind, rain and the Atlantic had all done their work. The foam had only just reached the hull each day but had been enough to spit over the keel before withdrawing and allowing the sun, before the rains came, to dry her out until the next high tide. At the same time, the locals had raised scavenging and beach combing to the levels of grand larceny and Salamander was now almost naked. They had left us with virtually nothing, but we begrudged them little. So many townspeople had shown us such kindness and generosity of spirit when they had little enough themselves, we were prepared to forgive the minority their spot of traditional opportunism.

Unemployment was a huge problem throughout Portugal and there were a dozen beggars scraping a living on the streets of Espinho with many more in Porto. The few factories in the area, making carpets, plastic goods and matches, had long queues of doleful young men lined up outside them every morning all hoping for a day's work. More often than not they were all turned away.

While George spent his hours, trousers rolled up, wading through the oily waters surrounding the engine and in the bilge, Tania and Kim played while Zoe and I alternately helped George or chased waves with the children and made the most of the cold, wet daylight. We had competitions to see who could follow the surf farthest down the beach before turning to run and avoid being soaked. The few Portuguese who ventured out on days like these, probably in the hope of picking another scrap from Salamander, had to settle instead for watching and waiting beneath the trees at the top of the beach. I hope they gained some solace from the reassurance that the English were, indeed, quite mad.

These watchers and waiters could never have been to the British seaside during one of our bank holidays. I well remember my father, sitting determinedly on a rented deckchair, arms folded, on Hastings beach. His eyes would fix on a point on the barely visible horizon, rain lashing down and his flat cap pulled firmly down over his ears. While the donkeys were gratefully led along the sands to shelter beneath the pier from the howling gale, we children were made to sit, turning blue and shivering, buckets and spades forgotten at our sides. Dad had paid his five bob for a day's hire of his deckchair and, by God, he was going to have his money's worth!

Unlike Hastings, however, after the great rolling Atlantic breakers had beaten the Portuguese coastline, huge terraces of sand were left piled against the rocks at one end of Espinho's beach. Like giant steps, each one three feet deep, they led up from the water's edge, leaning towards the cliffs. The girls soon found that if they stood on the edge of the highest of these temporary ridges, they could create their own personal avalanche. Together, they jumped then slid, hand in hand, shrieking with delight. They picked themselves up, sand glued to their clothes and jumped on the edge of the next ridge to slide down another level. So the game progressed until, eventually, they lay, flat on their backs, laughing, exhausted, spread out in the midst of a vast slope of freshly ploughed golden sand.

Our original estimate of being in Espinho for a couple of weeks had, we now realised, been ridiculously optimistic. I tried to convince myself that my high hopes had been for Zoe's sake, and had repeated them in my last postcard home to reassure my Mum. On 1st October I had written to her again. *'...Still here. It's not bad but would like to move on. We're still trying to sell everything but the pace here is so slow. I guess we'll be here a few weeks yet...'* My pen was working slower as well. I found myself writing small talk. I told her about a little boy, Pedro, who had made friends with the girls and how his parents had jokingly married him off to Tania.

There was no point worrying her with details of the misery we felt as we set about breaking Salamander up or the problems of dealing with Portuguese bureaucracy. She wanted to hear that we were well and the children were enjoying their holiday. *'...about half a mile from the house is a park for the children. It's amidst gardens and the play area is railed off with a man supervising all the time. The ground is covered with sand so it stops any nasty accidents. The kids think it's great so we go there most days...'*

She wouldn't want to know the real reason we went to the park every day. It would only worry her to know we were trying to ration ourselves to £1 a day, just to break even. If we exceeded our limit we would spend money faster than we were making it, although we were only buying basic necessities. If our financial situation continued as it was, we would never accumulate enough to get home. Mum wouldn't want to know that.

In addition to our salvage work, to keep our spirits up, we continued to plan our escape. Resigned to the unavoidable truth that we were now without a boat, we searched about for some other form of transport. The obvious answer was that we needed a car if, that is, we could find one that was large enough to carry three adults, two children and (hopefully) a lot of luggage. It also had to be cheap, but reliable enough to get us out of Portugal and through Spain without too many major disasters. We had heard the best place to buy second hand cars was Andorra.

The tiny independent State wedged into a valley of the Pyrenees between France and Spain had one great advantage over its neighbours. Like the Channel Islands, It didn't inconvenience itself by imposing too many taxes. If only Andorra were not landlocked, we might have contrived to be stranded there instead !

This enviable haven was, however, many miles away, especially bearing in mind that, even if we made the journey, there was no certainty of finding what we were looking for. Indeed, as things stood at the moment and however cheap their cars might be, it seemed unlikely that the small amount of cash we had would be enough.

We decided against risking any of our scarce resources on speculative journeys, instead putting the word out locally that we were in the market for a large, reliable (cheap) car. Meanwhile we continued to direct our energies to salvaging, selling, reducing the amount of luggage we would have to move and to finding alternative accommodation.

So far we had been lucky, in that we hadn't been pulled up for selling anything without being given permission. Now, however, we were being scrutinised much more closely and there was little point doing things that officials would later insist must be undone. According to John and Fernander, despite the official reassurances Jorge had obtained for us, there were still many potential pitfalls. Whatever we did, we could still be told after the event that we should have done things in a different way, or we should have had a permit, or it should not have been done at all.

When finally our gallant Saint Jorge reappeared to announce the arrival of his latest offspring, he brought with him a bottle of Champaign and the news that he could not yet reignite his battle with officialdom. His editor was sending him to attend a press convention in Coimbra. We could hardly complain. He poured the Champaign but looked quite upset when he saw our depressed and silent faces. George quickly reassured him we were delighted for him and drank a toast to the new arrival. Our depression was due only to the struggle against our financial tide. Jorge sighed deeply and put his glass down. He placed his fingers beneath his chin in a display of concentration we had seen several times before. At length, he sighed again, shrugged and suggested that, as there was nothing we could do for a few days, we might like to come with him to Coimbra. It was a nice place to visit and would make a change for us.

The town, he told us with an unexpected degree of precision, was 107 km. to the south. Because he had a tight schedule to keep, we would have to be ready to leave at 8 am and we might not get back until 11 pm. We thought of Tania and Kim with their tantrums and miseries after a long and busy day. This was the reason I often called them the little horrors, but despite that, we decided the opportunity to visit Coimbra outweighed the disadvantages.

The following morning we were all up bright and early and, by 8 o'clock sharp, were washed, dressed, fed and lined up for inspection.

An hour later, we were still waiting and the children were getting restless. A further 45 minutes ticked by before Jorge's car pulled up outside. Overcoming his initial surprise, he beamed at us, grateful, he said, that we were ready.

We didn't leave until 11.30. There always seemed to be time for a cup of coffee and a chat with John and Fernander or a neighbouring businessman or shop keeper before proceeding with the day's work. However laid back we thought he was, compared to most in Espinho, Jorge lived a whirlwind lifestyle.

The journey to Coimbra gave us a welcome glance at inland Portugal. Road building had not reached the high standards found in most of northern Europe and, combined with Jorge's break-neck driving, delivered a bumpy enough ride to please Kim and Tania, bouncing round on the back seat between me and Zoe.

Despite that, we enjoyed the scenery and Jorge's non-stop commentary and anecdotes about local people he knew in each of the villages we passed. When we arrived in the town, it hardly seemed possible that two hours had gone by since leaving Espinho.

Having made arrangements to meet Jorge later that evening, he dropped us off on the corner of a busy street near the centre of Coimbra. He pointed to an arched entrance set back from the pavement. This was one of the attractions he had told us about in the car.

Coimbra wasn't a large town; far smaller than Porto, but it was famous for its large plaster tableau depicting Portugal through the ages as well as its model village. As we approached the arch, Zoe stopped dead in her tracks, her mouth and eyes wide open.

At the entrance to the village stood six black guards, ten feet tall, their cold polished stone arms folded. Almost hypnotically, her hands rose in their direction as she approached them. Their inanimate, supercilious expressions gazed blindly as she hugged their broad limbs, fingering their shiny muscles moulded like sides of lean beef. The sheer bliss painted across her face reinforced what she had already told me about her fascination for tall muscular men.

Dragging her away and explaining with exaggerated patience that if she wanted a boyfriend she would have to find one that was a little shorter and, preferably, a little more alive, we started exploring the model village.

There was a castle, a playground, caves, pigs, ducks, sheep and, rather unexpectedly, a real aeroplane. In fact, everything that two small, very excited and impatient-to-enjoy-themselves girls could wish for.

There were churches decked out in full Catholic regalia, every detail faithfully reproduced in miniature. Around the walls of one of them, tiny blue and white ceramic tiles told stories from the Bible.

After calling at what seemed like every building in the little village at least twice, we meandered into Coimbra itself. This seemed quite a wealthy town by comparison to some we had seen, its main street boasting a smattering of elegant restaurants and hotels. The well stocked shops would have seemed even nicer, had we any money to spend in them. There again, we reasoned, a crystal chandelier and reproduction Louis XIV dining room suite would have looked rather out of place in the tent we were expecting to move into.

Having explored the town and beginning to feel the cold, we decided to visit the cinema. The film, like the last one we had seen, was in English with Portuguese sub-titles and was based on the story of the Onassis family. It was designated suitable only for children over 13 and the ticket clerk looked down rather doubtfully through her circular glass window at Kim and Tania. After discussion with the cinema manager they decided that, as the film was in a foreign language and we were foreigners, the children probably had a greater right than most to see it. We were allowed in. Their logic wouldn't have stood up to scrutiny, but we didn't argue.

George and I expected that after all the walking we had done, the girls would probably fall asleep anyway. To our surprise and some discomfort, they stayed awake. Our concerns faded when it became apparent that they weren't interested in the slightest by the bedroom scenes and asked no questions about words which (I hope) they hadn't heard before. Perhaps we were a little too sensitive about protecting our children.

We expected to come out of the cinema at about 10.30, which would have left just half an hour before our agreed rendezvous with Jorge. In the event, the film ended just before a quarter to nine and we emerged from the warm, cigarette smoked fug of the cinema into bitterly cold wind and rain. In desperation, we steeled ourselves to spend some more of our diminishing resources and spent the next hour and a half in a cafe.

As we approached the designated meeting point, Zoe placed her palms together in mock prayer and turned her eyes to the darkened sky.

"Please Jorge, just this once, please be on time."

The power of prayer !! There was our Saint Jorge, patiently waiting as promised, seated behind the wheel of his car and, as usual, reading one of his own articles in the newspaper. The relatively short journey home took a further two hours but the visit to Coimbra had made a welcome and interesting change.

We took another break from the tedium a few days later with a ride into Porto. Despite having made regular visits to the town over the last few weeks we always found it quite fascinating. The train journeys there and back invariably added to the entertainment. We had to cross a narrow bridge perched atop what seemed to be incredibly thin supports. It started 200 feet above the floor of a wide ravine and climbed another twenty feet before reaching the other side. At the bottom of the ravine trickled a lazy sludge of a river called the Douro, although we were told that when the rains arrived, the river would swell to a torrent. Many of the train crossings would have to be cancelled while maintenance workers strengthen the supports.

We wondered why, if this was such a predictable and regular event, the extra work wasn't put in hand during the summer when it would have been so much easier. We also wondered how we might survive if suddenly we were plunged 200 feet into the canyon below. Not surprisingly, perhaps, the little horrors seemed all the more excited by this prospect and each successive trip was accompanied by excited questions about whether we would go over the edge this time and would the bridge fall down now ?

The cost of this entertainment, compared to similar journeys (or fairground rides) at home, was minimal. A ticket costing around £10 would have taken one of us all the way to the Pyrenees. Had it not been for the need to transport all our worldly possessions with us, and the fact that we ultimately had to get back to Guernsey, we would have long before given up the idea of buying a car and settled for public transport. The unfortunate fact that French train tickets were then the most expensive in Europe, however, had swiftly despatched that idea to the 'non-starter' basket.

All over Porto were large and elaborate statues and memorials, erected during more prosperous times and now sadly neglected. Their railway station, a source of great civic pride due to its vast scale and engineering as well as its decoration, was covered in mosaic scenes from the area's history. I could have stayed there for hours, my imagination filling the gaps left in the stories they depicted. Tania and Kim, however, had other priorities – like food. Why is it that the smallest people in my family seem to have the largest appetites ?

Porto, we found, was a confused mix of squalid and discordant streets, wedged between magnificently regal public buildings and palatial private residences. The chasm between rich and poor was made all the more stark by their close proximity to each other.

The grandeur seemed quite obscene when, rounding a corner, we were assaulted by a stench of open sewers that physically pushed us backwards. The tiny, crumbling houses they served were occupied by swarms of swarthy black-haired Romany Portuguese. The women, all dressed in full pleated skirts and their men-folk in sharp grey suits which could have come straight from a wartime black market spiv, all seemed perfectly at ease in their squalid surroundings.

Their thick, glossy hair, oiled and smooth, made me quite envious as I looked at our flat, rain-soaked locks.

We passed them by and climbed several series of stone steps to a huge white stone building that Tania announced must be a palace. And everybody knew, where there was a palace, there had to be a fairy princess.

At the summit we sat on a long bench, surveying from this elevated viewpoint the cluttered town below. In these regal surroundings we chewed our way through our lunch, purchased for just under our £1 daily allocation, of bread rolls, apples, grapes and crisps, all washed down with a sweet sticky drink that may have been masquerading as orange juice.

It isn't every day one lunches at the palace.

The narrow streets below us were confused, filthy and untidy places. Laundry hung from every upstairs window and balcony, gathering fumes and grit from the traffic below. Despite this, the children were spotless, dressed for the start of their school term, the girls in bright white smocks and the boys in crisp clean shirts, all stiff with starch and the heat of a housewife's iron. Keeping themselves and their children clean seemed second nature to them while the education they were scrubbed and dressed for was given a rather lower priority. Their summer holiday, which they were now returning from, had begun at the beginning of June, over four months before.

We walked round the outside of the fairytale palace, telling each other stories of how the Princess within passed her time. She was either living happily ever after with a handsome Prince (with lots of ice cream and crisps, according to Tania) or, according to Zoe, was kept prisoner by her wicked uncle, locked in a dark cell and fed on mouldy bread.

Kim looked up, her eyes large and round. "Are there any rats ?"

Zoe nodded solemnly. "Lots."

I looked doubtfully down at my offspring, fearing a sleepless night.

Kim thought for a moment. "That's all right then. The rats will eat the mouldy bread instead of nibbling the Princess' toes and then they'll all go away and leave her alone." There was a pause as Kim assessed our need for further information. "Well, they'll want to find something nice to eat."

Just as we were running out of imagination, Kim asked whether we could "have another go on the train now." It seemed as good a time as any to make the trip home.

The journey back to Espinho was even more exciting than the outward trip. The train clattered down the steep rail bridge, gaining speed and shaking violently along the ancient rails. The wooden seats shifted below us as the retaining bolts, worn loose, moved with the vibration of the carriage. Although we tried to stop them, Kim and Tania flung their hands in the air and yelled as the train accelerated towards the first bend. It was something George had taught them when last we had taken them on a funfair big-dipper. I had told him at the time he would regret it.

We ran from the railway station to John and Fernander's house in the early evening rain, still giggling. We were greeted at the front door by Jorge. Unusually, he didn't seem pleased to see us and his sombre expression quickly dissolved what was left of our revelry. The news, he said solemnly, and somewhat unnecessarily, was not good.

The powers that be were demanding we pay £2,000. Apparently they wanted an advance on the tax they assumed would be due after Salamander and her salvaged contents and fittings were sold. Furthermore, we were required to remove her and everything else belonging to us from the beach, all within 28 days.

George was the first to collect his thoughts. "But we were given permission to sell the salvage before paying the tax. We signed an agreement." He tapped the palm of his hand with a thick finger. "They didn't say anything about a time limit or paying tax in advance."

Jorge shrugged. "That was the regional council. This letter," he waved it angrily, "is from the Federal State. They have over-ruled the mayor."

We sat round the table in silent consideration. If our garage proprietor took nearly everything we had, as agreed, the tax bill would pass largely to him. George looked optimistically across the table. Once again, Jorge looked uncomfortably glum. He shook his head. He had already spoken to him. On those terms, our buyer had indicated he was not interested. Whichever way we looked at it, the officials had us in a relentlessly crushing grip which they seemed intent on tightening. By trying to squeeze more cash out of us they had effectively removed our only opportunity of making a sale, and therefore our only means of paying them anything.

I looked plaintively at Jorge. "Is there nothing we can do?"

Another expansive shrug. "The best I can do is ask them to refer their decision to a judge."

This seemed a positively brilliant idea. Surely a fair minded judge would see things our way.

Jorge smiled patronisingly and shook his head. "It may delay them slightly. Nothing more."

Even giving Salamander away was no longer a viable proposition. Whoever took her on would be liable to pay the Government a sum that, for most people in the area, would be totally impossible.

As if to signal our disappointment, and as we sat wordlessly in Fernander's little kitchen, the noise of the rain beating against the windows grew more persistent. The winter rains had started in earnest and next week we were due to move into a tent.

It was then that I remembered. We had gone to Porto to buy a tent and cooking equipment but had completely forgotten to go to the camping shop. In addition to that, many of the things we had taken off Salamander with the idea of selling them had been stored in John's back yard. They were already saturated to the point of worthlessness or were beginning to rust.

My mind was taken back to a weekend camping trip we had taken the girls on a year or two before. We had always been perfectly prepared to 'rough it' and, young though they were, we thought a weekend in a friend's field would be good training for their future holidays. That weekend, it had rained – relentlessly and heavily. We had been swept out of our tent at three o'clock in the morning and spent the rest of the night draped over our friend's three piece suite. We still kept in touch with Angela, the proud owner of the field. Receiving a letter from her or other friends and family back in Guernsey was often the highlight of our week and kept us going through our gloomiest days spent in Espinho.

We were learning that Portugal was politically very unsettled and it seemed that every other day there was some rally or meeting held in the name of the People's Republic. Each time, business ground to a complete halt. Public holidays were called at every opportunity, enabling people to attend the rallies. In this way, the authorities fondly believed, the populace would become better informed and willingly participate in whatever activity the Government wished to promote.

It was on the eve of one such holiday that the garage owner formally and finally withdrew as a potential buyer. Along with that decision, he also withdrew his offer of help to remove the generator and other heavy chunks of hardware from beneath Salamander's deck. Our efforts to find another crane had to wait, delayed by several days public holiday. The local population first revelled then needed several days to recover while we simply had to wait until normality returned. We needn't have worried about the delay. We were eventually told the cost of hiring even a small portable crane started at £450. Scrap that idea.

When John suggested we try to borrow a pair of oxen from a local farmer we thought he was joking. In this strange land, however, which Lewis Carol's Alice might have found familiar, nothing could be taken for granted and nothing written off as too outlandish.

As the rain beat down we continued, hopelessly, for hour after sodden hour, to rescue items of clothing and dry them out. No sooner had Zoe and I got one set of clothes dry than Tania or Kim would appear, hair matted to their heads, arms outstretched and waterlogged, dripping across Fernander's floor, asking pathetically to be dried out.

The local orphanage to which we hoped to hand on many of their redundant clothes and toys had closed for another in a long string of holidays. During these times the children were farmed out to an army of volunteer foster parents and the managers of the orphanage were nowhere to be found. Until it re-opened most of our small storage space was used up by the bags and bundles we had set aside for them. We tried selling some of our other clothes but the local people were even poorer than we were ! Those few who could afford second hand clothes were only prepared to part with a few pence.

Having worked out we had just enough money left to buy a tent, haversacks and sleeping bags from an army surplus store, we agreed to give away as much as we could, if only to lighten the load.

By following this course, we would use up the last of our cash. Any chance to buy a car and drive home would disappear with it. However, there was no car available and even if there had been, we doubted that we would have also been able to afford the petrol.

If we moved onto the camp site, we would have to sell items of far greater value than we had managed so far. Only then would we be able to pay any of the £2,000 tax (which seemed ludicrously optimistic, even after Jorge's delaying tactic) as well as buy a car and still leave enough to support ourselves during the journey home.

We bit the bullet, convinced that our luck had to change, and went shopping. We had done our sums correctly. The English money we had was exactly enough to pay for the tent.

The other things, though, essential to life under canvas, would cost a further £60 which we didn't have. We brazened it out, assuring the shop owner there was no problem. We would call back in a couple of hours with the full amount.

Back at John's house, he once again proved our faith in human kindness by offering to buy the tent along with everything else we needed. We couldn't possibly accept after his generosity over the previous month and determined to scrape together the necessary money ourselves.

The short delay we had promised at the army surplus shop turned into three days. This seemed entirely in keeping with the Portuguese understanding of such things and caused no surprise at all when finally we returned and made our purchases.

We trekked off to the camp site, still in driving rain. Now saturated to the point that sheltering from a downpour had become a wholly pointless exercise, we strolled at our leisure round the site, inspecting each plot and assessing it for size, position and aspect.

A major consideration was the slope of the land and every minor rivulet of rainwater was closely studied for direction and volume. Finding a pitch which met most of our requirements, Zoe suggested digging a canal along the upper side of the plot and then down the line of the hill to drain the water away from the tent.

George nodded thoughtfully. There was just one problem. We hadn't foreseen the ferocity of Portugal's latest cloudburst – or Zoe's inventive solution – so hadn't bought a shovel. George began ferreting through our belongings in search of a substitute. At length, he produced three table spoons and a small pink plastic spade that Tania had managed to hide while we were selecting gifts for the orphanage.

He stuck one of the spoons into the grass and levered a small plug of green fringed mud out of the ground. Wordlessly, Zoe and I followed suit, oblivious to the fact that our labours were making absolutely no difference to the direction or behaviour of the gallons of rain water washing over our small patch of soil.

Zoe's spoon made a loud sucking noise followed by the plop of a rubber plunger being pulled from a blocked plughole. Suddenly realising the futility of what we were doing, we fell to uncontrollable giggling. If our cynical friends – those who had tried to discourage us from leaving Carey Cottage – could see us now...

Nevertheless, our selected plot was within hailing distance of three other tents and a small touring caravan. At least we wouldn't be entirely without company. Perhaps they were homeless as well. What other reason could anyone have for camping in a monsoon ?

We battled with the soaking canvas and poles for a full hour before finally George was satisfied with the result. However irritating his pedantic perfectionism in the midst of a howling downpour, we knew he was right to be so particular. Had the poles been at the wrong angle or the guy ropes to loose, as any regular camper will confirm, the canvas roof would have quickly become a rain catcher and bowed under the weight. In a matter of a few hours the whole structure would have come crashing in on itself.

Tired but triumphant, we returned to John and Fernander's house, our spirits decidedly brighter than the weather. We even joked about where we would hang out our washing (to rinse, not to dry) and where to build the patio to take greatest advantage of the evening sun. (There was a sun up there somewhere, wasn't there ?). Our various decisions having been made, the tent purchased and pitched, we felt progress had been made.

Saint Jorge was waiting for us, his halo gleaming even more brightly than usual. He slapped a small bunch of keys on the table in front of us and announced that, for a token rent, we could now become the tenants of a fine three bedroom apartment in an up-town area of Espinho.

We sat, once again momentarily silenced by the rapidity of change in our fortunes. I broke the lull.

"But we've just bought a tent."

Jorge closed his eyes and shook his head. "You will not need it."

"But we've picked our plot on the camp site." Zoe insisted.

"You will not need that either."

"But we've just put the tent on it."

"Then you may take it down again."

Tania added her own argument. "But we made a special river for the rain and everything."

Possibly Jorge didn't understand this entirely obvious reference, but the pure serenity and undeniable logic of his words gave us no room to argue – even if we had wanted to.

I turned to Zoe, tears welling up. I was so pleased, especially for her. She had put up with a lack of privacy for so long.

Although she had never mentioned it, I knew that my little horrors, who gave her no peace, along with my chattering and the unspeakable noises which emanated from both ends of George throughout the night, had all been keeping her awake.

Once again, we packed up our gear. As George went back to the site to dissemble the meticulous tent, Zoe and I cleaned our little room. I found myself silently praying that we would never have to move again; a pointless hope, given our present circumstances.

We settled into our new home; a veritable palace by comparison to the accommodation we had become used to and the canvas covering we had been anticipating. The apartment belonged to Jorge's parents who had bought it many years before when property prices had hit rock bottom. It was, said Jorge, an investment for their retirement but they occasionally let it out for a few weeks during the summer. Suddenly life didn't seem too bad after all. As if to prove the point, Tania reminded me that, over the last few weeks, she had learned to swim and to ride a bike. These great achievements were as nothing, however, to her proudest boast. In the last three days she had announced the arrival of two new teeth !

We now decided we could organise ourselves better. We prepared advertisements of all we had to sell, translated for us by Fernander and, feeling guilty that I had written so few letters home, now had sufficient good news to justify the cost of more stamps and postcards.

Our standard of living rose dramatically. After sleeping on the floor for a month, our first night's sleep in a real bed was total luxury. The fact that we were eating almost exclusively out of tins bought during my giant shopping spree in Guernsey mattered not a jot. I have never been an enthusiastic cook and that aspect of our existence suited me perfectly.

The strange phenomenon of evaporating tins had not thus far caused us too much concern either. Whether they had been in the holds aboard Salamander or placed temporarily on the beach, a multitude of boxes containing our larder had strangely disappeared since our arrival in Espinho. It would have seemed churlish, in view of the generosity of the people in the village, to make an issue of it with the local Police. It was unlikely they would have done anything about it in any case. However poverty stricken we thought we were, the people we now shared our lives with had only ever known this sort of hardship. The day had not yet come when George and I would deny them a tin of baked beans !

To celebrate our turn of good fortune, we returned to a little cafe close the beach where Salamander lay. The café owner had shown us immediate and unconditional friendship when we had first landed on his doorstep (almost literally !) His immediate offer of a variety of hot and cold drinks had been more than welcome. His café seemed to barely survive, both physically and financially. Built of rough timber, it sold only beer, local wine and thick black Espresso coffee and was supported by a trickle of loyal regular customers. The chances are, the majority of them spent most of their waking hours there but spent little more than a few Escudos a day.

To show our gratitude we took him a bottle of gin, raised from the depths of the cavernous hold that had protected it from Tweedledum and Tweedledee.

The café owner didn't understand, at first, that it was a gift. Finally realising we wanted no payment, he was immediately overcome with emotion, first hugging the bottle to his chest then gazing adoringly at the label. He rehearsed with carefully intoned pronunciation before articulating out loud the mantra "Gordon's Dry Gin". He repeated the words several times before serving us all with drinks, flatly refusing any payment, then disappearing from sight below the rough plank that was his counter.

When he reappeared, he was clutching two crumpled brown paper bags which, with much ceremony and sombre bowing, he presented to Kim and Tania. They thanked him politely and, peering into the bags, announced they were sweets. Tania's hand was already diving into the depths of her bag but, as neither of them had yet had their lunch, we persuaded them to drink their lemonade for the moment and save their presents for later.

During the walk home, finally relenting, we conceded they could each have a sweet to keep them going (and keep them quiet).

I forget which of the girls squealed either first or loudest, but it was just as well we were well out of earshot of the café. They each held up a red boiled sweet, adhering to their fingers like a swollen blushing limpet. Recovering from the initial shock, Kim inspected hers closely, eyes crossing as she brought it closer to her nose. Tania opted for a safer route and pushed hers towards my face, her arm outstretched, strange gagging noises emitting from the back of her throat.

Both sweets were covered in goo ridden red ants, all glued firmly and finally to the saccharine orbs. Not easily defeated in matters of confection, the girls shook the sweets from their fingers and dipped back into their bags. Each time their fingers withdrew, becoming stickier at each dip, the motionless adhesive ants came with them.

Whether they had died of exhaustion or saccharine overdose we will never know. Only when the girls came to open their packets of crisps, thoughtfully placed beneath the semi liquid sweets, were any of the dead insects' surviving brothers and sisters discovered. Potato starch and salt, apparently, is not so lethal a mixture to an ant as artificial sweetener. Their tiny legs beat up and down the girls' hands, flitting between the remaining specks of sugar mixture.

Fortunately, we were still walking along the beach and a swift and thorough dunking in the sea quickly ended their encounter. We walked the remainder of our journey home with two small and very dissatisfied girls, their sulks barely alleviated by frequent promises of replacement goody bags.

Despite all this, our new home lifted our spirits. Such was our feeling of well-being that even the next bulletin from local officials, delivered as usual by Jorge, failed to drag us down. In addition to the £2,000 tax bill, the authorities had now decided to fine us £1,000 unless we removed Salamander from the beach within the next seven days.

"But we've only just been told we had 28 days." George stared in disbelief at the letter, still in Jorge's hand.

It was another opportunity for Jorge to exercise his well practised shrug. "This is the local council getting revenge on the Federal Government for over-ruling them."

Patiently, Jorge explained that when the ruling by the local mayor's office had been overturned, the local council had lost their share of our tax revenue. A fine for littering, however, came entirely within their jurisdiction.

Without being asked, Saint Jorge promised to visit the mayor personally and persuade him that we no more had £1,000 than we had the wherewithal to move a 97 ft. boat.

Three days later, granted an audience, we stood in a neat row behind our mentor, Fernander whispering a translation in my ear. Before us, the rotund mayor sat behind a large polished walnut desk, disinterestedly fingering the mayoral sash which crossed his chest.

If we had owned such a sum, Jorge told the implacable politician, we would have been able to employ the necessary manpower to take Salamander off the beach well before now. That is, if such a feat had been humanly possible. Jorge leant forward, his knuckles resting on the polished wood. Even the mighty Portuguese Navy, the finest Navy in Europe... The Mayor coughed behind his hand. Jorge corrected himself. The finest Navy in the world. Even they, after all, had not been up to the task. How could his worship expect us, mere foreigners, with our limited resources, to succeed where the world finest had failed ?

His impassioned speech and lucid argument, apparently, left the bureaucrats unmoved. The Mayor apologised with an insincere flick of his fingers. The order had been signed and the official paper stamped along with the official foot. The Mayor's office would not be moved. Impasse.

Outside on Porto's main street, our 15 minute audience over, we asked Jorge what he thought we should do. He gave yet another of his well accustomed shrugs.

"There is nothing we can do. It is more a question of what they can do."

Not for the first time, we had no control over our immediate future. We had no choice but to wait for the answer to Jorge's question; wait for buyers and wait for the orphanage to re-open.

We decided to explore the area a little more. After all, the more we looked, the more likely we were to come across something or somebody who might be able to help.

Not all of our explorations, it has to be said, were as culturally uplifting as our visits to Porto and Coimbra. We leafed through a small collection of large scale maps that Zoe's Mum had kindly sent us, selected one at random and opened it across the kitchen table.

Zoe placed a hand across her eyes. Her hand circled briefly above the sheet and she allowed her finger to drop onto the map. We all looked down, focussing on her fingertip.

"Picoto." Zoe read the small print, squinting closely as the tiny speck sandwiched between contour lines. A single dotted line denoted the minor road winding through it.

A friendly neighbour who owned an old Ford truck was summoned. He looked at each of our hopeful expressions in turn and scratched his head. In his broken English he asked why we could possibly want to visit Picoto.

"We think the name sounds nice." Zoe smiled, the logic unassailable. The neighbour shook his head. It was only 12 kilometres away. He was more than happy to give us a lift.

We rattled out of Espinho and shortly turned up a rough track. I looked over my shoulder, wedged between George and the driver in the front of the truck. Through a grimy window directly behind our heads, Zoe was sitting in the open back with the girls, tracing our route from them on her map. They giggled with every bounce and swerve, enjoying another fairground ride.

Their laughter turned to shrieks as the driver rammed on the brakes to avoid a goat straying across the road before slamming his foot on the accelerator again. Another few stomach churning swerves and we pulled up at the side of the road.

He stuck his hand out of the window, palm upwards. "Picoto." He announced. We looked around doubtfully, seeing nothing but open scrubland. Dazed, and too embarrassed to question him, we piled out of the truck. Our driver happily swung a wide U-turn across the rough field and disappeared round the last bend, his left hand still waving cheerily from the window. We concluded we must have been left somewhere outside the village. We walked on, seeking the bright lights and entertainment we felt sure this new metropolis had to offer.

For three miles, we found nothing more captivating than a scarcely visited and run down petrol station. Its attendant, leaning back on an old kitchen chair, barely glanced up as we walked by trying to look as though we knew where we were. We nodded and spoke a brief greeting. He said nothing. Round the next bend, tantalisingly, stood a small café, denoted by its single table and two chairs set at the side of the road. Getting closer, hearts falling, we saw its door was firmly closed and bolted. Next to it, a shelter which might originally have been erected for the local goats but which even they seemed now to have snubbed.

As ever, we were left with little alternative; we turned and retraced our steps. It was, at least, down hill most of the way. This time, we didn't acknowledge the garage owner but were conscious of his eyes following our backs down the road.

It was four hours before we crawled back into Espinho, foot sore but a little wiser about our local surroundings. Strike Picoto off the sight-seeing itinerary !

The following day we spent recovering, lazily (and guiltily) dozing. Zoe, on the other hand, exhibiting extraordinary energy, busied herself baking magnificent fruit tarts. Needless to say my embarrassment and guilt quickly dissolved when she placed the gently steaming tray on the table in front of us.

To cap the day, Saint Jorge arrived and, finding us draped lethargically over the furniture, offered to take us all out for the evening.

Café Enfante was his 'local,' run by an extended family who Jorge clearly knew well. He introduced us to a confusing multitude of brothers, sisters, uncles, aunts and cousins before ordering a round of drinks. In our woefully domestic way, we expected the children to be offered soft drinks. Wrong again ! We looked on with a mixture of anxiety and fascination as the little horrors, delighted at their sudden promotion to adulthood, sipped peppermint liqueurs laced with lemonade. Jorge could barely comprehend our disquiet over combining small children with strong alcohol.

Our evening out escalated unexpectedly when, without warning, the entire family rose and moved towards the door.

They ushered us ahead of them and into a fleet of waiting cars.

Blindly, we allowed ourselves to be driven out of the narrow village streets and into the surrounding countryside. Jorge had placed himself behind the wheel of one of the other cars and we had no way of asking any of our fellow travellers where we were going. Zoe claimed to recognise a few landmarks but, I had to admit, in the moonless gloom I found it hard to identify anything.

The rain still beating a tattoo on the car roof, we swung round several bends before we caught sight of something we all recognised. Ahead of us was a large grey building which we knew lay on the outskirts of Porto. Bright floodlights now illuminated the grey stone of the building's façade but, despite its dominating aspect, we had never discovered its purpose during any of our previous visits.

Quite out of place, it had all the appearance of a Georgian town hall. Tall Greek pillars lined the front of the building, raised from the street by a series of broad steps. Romanesque statues stood in alcoves along its front wall, gazing out into the blinding floodlights.

A long queue snaked from the far end of the street, moving slowly up the steps and culminating in an excited jostling crowd, encased by the large open doorframe. We negotiated the queue, becoming bathed in the light within, emanating from chandeliers hanging from the high ceiling above the foyer. Only then did we realise the treat we had been invited to enjoy.

Banners hung from elaborate plaster mouldings on the walls, announcing we had been brought to an international four-way Roller Hockey competition. The protagonists were Espinho, Porto, Lisbon and the Spanish national side, on the first leg of a European tour.

The excitement built to a crescendo whenever either of the local teams put in an appearance. When the Porto players, who seemed to have encouraged most of the town to turn out in support, beat Lisbon with a last minute goal, the noise from the crowd, already deafening, threatened to shake the old building to the ground. Drums thundered, Klaxons blared and great showers of confetti and paper streamers poured onto the pitch. It was far more important that a local side had beaten the team from the national capital than any result against the touring Spaniards.

Espinho, always the underdogs, were narrowly beaten by Porto but put up a strong enough fight against both Lisbon and the Spaniards to merit several standing ovations. At the end of the evening they were at the bottom of the points table, but honour had been well served and their fans went home satisfied.

Kim and Tania were absolutely transfixed by the whole occasion. Bearing in mind the games didn't start until 9 pm and went on until midnight, it must have been fate that had made them sleep for most of the morning following our marathon of the previous day.

We emerged from the sports hall, tired but delighted to have experienced a local pastime filled with passion. As we were carried back to Espinho, the discussion raced unabated on the subject of Roller Hockey; a subject which, under Jorge's expert tutelage, we now considered ourselves quite expert.

We were still gabbling about the merits of the forward flip, the reverse shuffle and dummy pass as we poured from Jorge's car into Café Enfante. We cared not a jot that it was now well after midnight.

Café Enfante became George's trading centre as he attempted to sell off bits of Salamander. He would regularly arrange to meet potential customers there to discuss their needs before taking them for a viewing. Usually, the meeting was set for 6 pm and, just as usually, the buyer would appear at around 10 pm. George soon learned the Portuguese way of doing business and often consumed several dishes of food and bottles of wine before negotiations were permitted to commence.

Meeting late in the evening, however, had a strange advantage. We discovered that the policemen placed on sentry duty with Salamander were seldom there late at night, despite telling us they would be – and being ordered to be by their superiors. It was their purpose, they had assured us, to protect us from looters. We had been assured they were there to protect our property but their true purpose, we suspected, was to monitor what we salvaged. They were frequently seen completing official forms; a clear sign that the information was being passed to officials who, as if by coincidence, would appear a few days later, clip board and tax demand in hand.

George became accustomed to inspecting and removing items by torch light after the officers had slipped away to their favourite bar. Those few, sufficiently worried about losing their jobs, remained on the beach late into the night. They could generally be persuaded to look the other way at the relevant moment if offered a bottle of Whisky.

My early fears that being caught in possession of a hold stuffed full of strong liquor would land us in trouble with the authorities had been absolutely, totally and wonderfully unfounded.

While George had been learning his new trade of black marketeer, the rest of us, within a relatively short passage of time, had slipped into a weekly routine. Mondays had become our 'treat days' as we were able to visit Porto market. The treat, of course, had nothing to do with the grind of buying fruit and veg. Our favourite stall was at the far end of the market. It was here that we could indulge ourselves with hot sugared doughnuts.

These were deep fried in the usual way, but the dough was first pressed out into a flat sheet then rolled into long tubes. After cooking, they were dipped in syrup until they were full to overflowing and sprinkled with fine sugar. Finally, they were cut into three inches long segments with a large pair of rusty scissors. They may not have looked like doughnuts, but their taste made market days special !

We got into the habit of making a bee-line for the doughnuts first, convincing ourselves that if we waited until after we had done our shopping it would be too difficult to hold our bags and doughnuts at the same time. As the delightful confection cost no more than a few pence and we had two voracious infant appetites to satisfy as well as our own, we invariably found ourselves returning for a second helping after touring less exciting tables of cabbages, potatoes and apples.

Between all this heady high living, the less enjoyable part of our week involved constant sorting and re-sorting of our worldly possessions. These exercises were punctuated by occasional surprise discoveries and on one occasion we found a hearing aid which at one time had belonged to

George's mother. When next we saw him, we asked Jorge to find a deserving recipient.

Within the hour Jorge returned with a teenage lad who had been almost totally deaf since childhood. Jorge translated his almost tearful words of gratitude. He inserted the hearing aid in his better ear and, miraculously, found both it and the battery still worked. He could hear voices for the first time in years. They were muffled, he said, but he could understand if people spoke slowly. Most of all, he could hear and enjoy the music he loved so much. He grasped my hands in his, speechlessly shaking his head and blinking back tears.

Saint Jorge later explained the youngster couldn't understand how people who he had been told were foreigners, stranded with no money, could be so generous. In Portugal the cost of a hearing aid would have cost the equivalent of several months pay. He had long given up any hope that he would ever be able to hear again.

We thanked our patron saint for finding so worthy a recipient. The incident renewed our resolve to dig out anything and everything which could of benefit to any of the local people. As we kept saying, the less we had to carry, the quicker we could move. Jorge was satisfied with the outcome for a quite different reason. He instinctively knew that here lay the follow-up story he and his editor had been waiting for.

A few days later the headline splashed across the local newspaper's front page read *'Marooned Britons Give Espinho Youth A New Chance In Life.'* Perhaps it had been a slow news day, but we and Saint Jorge were all happy with the result.

Despite these fulfilling moments, much of our time was spent in sheer frustration. Zoe, Kim, Tania and I spent many hours wandering aimlessly round the town, seeking activities to occupy ourselves – and our little horrors – while George spent his days even more frustratingly. Hours at a time were spent pacing about the apartment or sitting in Café Enfante waiting for Jorge to deliver news from one government ministry or another or for buyers to arrive, albeit seldom with any money in their pockets.

So immersed were we that we had completely forgotten that our Saint Jorge had a job, a wife and a young family, which now included Isabel, their new daughter of three weeks.

Nevertheless, when the next official indicated he wished to interview us, Jorge was there at our side to translate and negotiate. The young man placed a copy of the local newspaper on the table between us, smoothing Jorge's front page headline with the back of his hand. He rattled off a sentence in rapid Portuguese.

Jorge coughed, embarrassed. "The officer wishes to know the value of the hearing aid."

We looked at each other blankly, then at Jorge. "It is a taxable item, apparently."

The indignation in my voice was unmistakeable, even to a young tax inspector who didn't understand English. "But it was a gift. We gave it away."

Another of Jorge's shrugs. "I know. He knows." He thrust a thumb at the official. There was another animated Portuguese exchange, the official tapping the newspaper article and Jorge slapping first the table, then his forearm in a gesture, we presumed, of contempt. The official took out a note pad and scribbled a column of figures, underlining the last number several times.

Jorge leant across the table, tore the page off the notepad, crumpled it up and tossed it over his shoulder. More gesticulating, raised voices and arm slapping. Finally, the official, red faced and exasperated, pulled out his final weapon, a pad of tax demand forms which in firm strokes he started to fill in.

Jorge waved his hands over the page, turning to us, as if we needed an explanation. "I tell him. There is no point. This demand for tax is false. It is nonsense."

The form completed, it was carefully lifted from the pad, folded neatly and handed to George. Jorge snatched it away, tore it into several strips and tossed them into the air. As they fluttered down, the tax man, muttering darkly, packed his pen and forms away. He stood, then bowed briefly and with exaggerated courtesy, first to George, then to me. He shouted a final insult at Jorge and stormed out of the apartment.

We sat in silence for a few minutes, gazing at the confetti dotted across the table. It was Jorge who spoke first. "It's OK. He's a very junior man. No important."

The tax bill had been judged to be £100; a measure of how much the Portuguese hard of hearing had to pay for a hearing aid. Jorge assured us we would hear no more about it.

Spurred on by the success of the hearing aid and preferring Jorge's assessment of the tax question to the official one, Zoe and I scooped up the large pile of children's clothes that had been occupying the corner of one of the bedrooms and pushed them into a bag.

The little horrors had not allowed our situation to hamper their growth rate and since leaving Guernsey had shot up by several inches. This rapid development had convinced us that disposal of their old clothes was the only sensible course. Many of their jumpers could no longer be forced over their heads and when the zips of trousers and skirts were stretched to breaking point, the time had come to find a wearer of more suitable size.

In the park we often went to we had seen a young girl with two smaller children, a boy and a girl, twins perhaps, of about three years old.

The collective eyes of this little group changed in unison as we approached. First casual disinterest, followed by concern as they realised we were approaching them. This turned to curiosity then, finally, some sort of understanding. They seemed quite pleased with our offerings and we left the older girl rummaging through the bag, experimentally holding shorts, T-shirts and sundry items of winter clothing against each of the twins.

It was now 31st October and just as we came to the morose conclusion that the sale of Salamander's salvage had all but ground to a halt, Saint Jorge rode in on his white charger again.

He called to the apartment to break the news that he had found someone interested in buying the generator and compressor. He had also learned that there was a car for sale which might suit us. It was a seven year old Opel Rekord and quick calculations confirmed that if we could raise £900 we could close the deal. It was owned by an elderly man living locally who now felt it was too large and expensive to run. He had often been heard loudly complaining that the cost of petrol had climbed too steeply and that his insurance company had put their premiums up because, he suspected, they believed he was getting too old to drive. He had determined to go the way of the majority of Portuguese motorists and find a car which ran on diesel – along with a right minded insurance company.

Having said that, part of the cost of motoring must have been due to the way the Portuguese drove. Accelerator peddles spent most of their short lives rammed to the floor and engines were regularly revved to pieces. At least this national pastime seemed to support the local economy, generating work for garage mechanics called upon to overhaul engines as often as most people emptied their car's ashtrays !

The Opel's owner, however, had assured Jorge (and everyone else he thought might be remotely interested in buying his car) that this was not so in his case. He seldom drove at all and when he did, it was with meticulous care. He had owned the car from new and it had been regularly serviced. Bearing in mind our recent experiences with engines and all things mechanical, George was suitably suspicious. At my insistence, he assured me that he would inspect it thoroughly before making any decision.

Despite this, George was eager to open negotiations straight away. If this was to be our means of leaving Portugal, it was an opportunity not to be missed. We nodded decisively and told Jorge we would go and visit the Opel the following morning.

Jorge gave us one of his broad, smiling shrugs. The next day was a national day of mourning and had been declared a public holiday. Nothing could be done for a few days. The population would spend their time in their local churches and cemeteries, scrubbing them, polishing the marble and stonework, arranging flowers and mourning their dead. Salvage and car sales would have to wait.

Setting our frustration aside once again, we scanned the map in search of somewhere new to explore. We decided on the little village of Silualde. As usual, our choice was based on nothing more than curiosity and a liking for the sound of the name. The day being a holiday, there were no buses or trains running and, again, we were given a lift by a neighbour.

Like Porto, Silualde was packed with examples of horrendous poverty rubbing shoulders with flamboyant displays of wealth.

The weather, at least, felt decidedly British. A chill wind reminded us of a northern winter but even when accompanied by a smattering of rain, failed to prevent the local children from paddling along the streets. Bare footed, they played between foraging cats and scratching dogs. Chickens, scrawny and drab, pecked pointlessly at the gutters in search of a living.

Front doors, long since rotted and removed from their hinges, were now replaced by forlorn bits of old sacking. They gave little protection from the elements, intent on destroying the sad bits of laundry that hung limply from lines strung along the fronts of their houses.

Along the weather beaten sea front, a few fishing boats sat on the beach. Always a source of interest to George, we wandered past them, pausing occasionally to inspect a piece of rigging or other hardware. Could it be that one of these small vessels would benefit from a bit of Salamander. It seemed unlikely. George had already commented, with some surprise, that none of them had an engine or even a sail. Up to 40 feet in length, they relied entirely on the rowing power of their owners and crew. These were sailors who knew everything they needed to know about the behaviour of fish and sea, but nothing of engines or generators. They had never used them and never would. Such knowledge was entirely unnecessary. A few boat owners were using the holiday as an opportunity to repair their nets sat under makeshift tarpaulin shelters. They barely looked up as we passed.

One in particular crouched in the dim light, a damp cigarette in one corner of his mouth and large darning needle in the other. Bending low over his work and squinting from beneath the wrinkled peak of his denim cap, he threaded the twine skilfully, his fingers working no less dextrously than a Belgian lace maker. George paused to watch briefly, his head shaking involuntarily in admiration. The fisherman, feeling the feint shadow we were casting, looked up. Recognising a kindred spirit, he removed the damp cigarette and nodded politely to George before continuing his work.

We ended up, as we had so often during past explorations of this kind, sitting in a little church at the centre of the village.

Despite the local florists raising their prices three-fold overnight in time for the national day of mourning, the shrines around the little church were festooned with cut flowers. Ferns and orchids, lovingly placed amongst the candles, lanterns and even candelabras gave the place a strangely festive feel.

The figures of Christ and His Saints looked down on us as we sat in silence, each scrape of Kim or Tania's shoe or shuffle of bored bottom on the wooden pew echoed eerily above our heads.

As a devout agnostic I can do without the blood and gore employed on the high Church's more gruesome representations of the crucifixion, but my agnosticism was shaken that morning. The hair on the back of my neck prickled and stood spikily to attention. Uneasily, I rose from my seat and walked to the side of the church. Each time I glanced up at the crucified Christ above the altar, I could have sworn His eyes had followed me.

Whether the statue's eyes were moving or not, something in the little church definitely was. A few feet from us sat a dark and swarthy Romany family. They knelt in prayer, their fingers so tightly linked together their knuckles blanched through the suntanned skin. The man, smartly dressed in sombre suit and tie, seemed distracted from his devotions, frequently breaking off to scratch his head. As I moved back to our place in the pew, I glanced down at the back of their bowed heads. His hair, plastered flat with oil, was alive with lice.

Hastily, I tapped George on the shoulder and beckoned. We moved on.

George's usual protests at visiting churches cemeteries had been quickly quashed on this occasion. This time he hadn't been able to use his often exercised excuse that he had to wait at the apartment for news or go on one of his foraging expeditions to the beach. Ironically, it might have been the one occasion when, had we known about the occupants of the supplicants' hair, we would have stayed away.

I had long tired of complaining that George spent his evenings with Journalist Jorge and John at Café Enfante, quaffing large quantities of wine and spirits. I knew what his answer would be, and knew too that he was telling the truth. Barely a day went by when the possibility of a potential buyer didn't draw him to the café. It seemed business deals were impossible without the expedient of large quantities of alcohol consumed into the early hours of the morning.

Thus far, George had only occasionally returned with confirmation that anything had been sold. He would far more frequently appear at around two or three o'clock in the morning, slightly although seldom dangerously the worse for a night of drinking. He would smile expansively, offering a bottle of Port in each hand. "I know I'm late," he would say, pouring each of us a generous measure, "but wait 'til I tell you what happened ..."

More often than not, nothing of any consequence had happened. All he brought back with him were tales of the meals Jorge had persuaded him to sample. These seemed to consist, in the main, of squid cooked and served in their own 'ink' or pigeon, sparrow, a highly suspect variety of black pudding or chicken intestines, heads and feet. These were often supplemented by a selection of shrivelled up and heavily spiced sausages, the origin of which was never revealed. At least, though, I acquired a taste for Portuguese Port. Even today, I find it easier to drink if taken sitting up in bed during the early hours of the morning.

Whether or not such lengthy meetings produced any solid results, other than indigestion, was largely immaterial. If we wanted to sell any of our salvage, Jorge assured us, George had to be available to negotiate. If he wasn't there, potential buyers would take their custom somewhere else. I had no idea there were other marooned travellers competing for our trade.

If nothing else, his regular appearances at the café had proved Journalist Jorge's early promise that George had become a local celebrity. We couldn't walk down the street without some shopkeeper or other hailing us with a wave and a "Hola – Capitano !"

These would be accompanied by much shoulder patting, hand shaking and generous donations of large bags of fruit and vegetables. We neither understood their words of encouragement nor their generosity, but we were always grateful. The people of Espinho loved children, and we couldn't take the girls for a walk through the village without running a gauntlet of elderly women and shopkeepers wielding bags of sweets and chocolate. Our meagre resources would have expired far sooner without their continuous and unsolicited good will.

So great was the welcome given us that the longer we stayed in Espinho, the greater the risk became that we would stumble into the rut that had kept us for so long in our comfortable home on Guernsey.

As witness to this possibility, we soon got into the habit, each Friday, of visiting John and Fernander for an evening meal. We had come to call these our 'frango' evenings. Frango is the Portuguese for chicken and as a result we could always depend on at least one wonderfully cooked hot meal each week.

They supplied the food – chicken, of course, cooked especially for the family in hot, spiced wine by an Indian restaurant a few doors away and served with fresh rolls and chestnuts. We supplied the wine (cold and unspiced) which, at 20 pence a bottle, flowed in quantity !

The repast always ended with chestnuts, roasted to perfection in their wood fuelled oven. Various relations, neighbours, friends and other members of the household would attend these banquets and at least three chickens, a large bag of chestnuts and several bottles were always needed.

The routine was broken only by festival days when we were issued with additional invitations to Sunday evening 'typically Portuguese' meals. Frango, apparently, was not the only dish on the national menu. I didn't know whether I was going to laugh or cry when we were told what it was. I could hear Zoe choking back her giggles behind me and I didn't dare look at George. If he had so much as smirked I would have been helpless.

"I had no idea," I eventually managed to say, "that boiled tripe and trotters were a Portuguese delicacy." Sometimes I thought that John must have been living in Espinho too long.

As usual, the meal was thoroughly enjoyed by a broad spectrum of friends, family and neighbours who seemed to appear from nowhere each time a dish was brought to the table.

Following the meal, we all migrated yet again to Café Enfante for copious quantities of booze, fruit juice, coffee, sweets and a variety of snacks that were devoured with such relish that nobody would have believed we had already spent over four hours eating.

During most of our visits, though, John and Fernander tried to make us feel at home with cuisine that was more English than Portuguese. It might seem ungrateful but there is only so much rice and pasta one can eat and still enjoy. Even Café Enfante took to providing us with toasted ham and cheese sandwiches.

They apologised repeatedly that they had no facilities to provide our British national dish. After the fourth or fifth such apology, I asked Fernander what it was they felt unable to provide, naively suggesting I might try to correct the situation.

"Fish and chips, of course." Fernander grinned impishly. "I told them whenever I visit John's family this is all we eat."

I opened my mouth to object but Fernander swiftly admitted she might have exaggerated slightly. On reflection I realised fish and chips would be more than welcome, provided, of course, they were served in newspaper with plenty of salt and vinegar. I had never been able to make batter and suddenly wished I had paid more attention during that particular domestic science lesson. The Channel Islands and south coast of England being well supplied with fish and chip shops, I had never felt the need to learn.

Sharing John and Fernander's small house was Emma. She was 21 but looked much younger. She was some sort of distant relation to Fernander and they gave her work as a cleaner. She found a kindred spirit in Zoe and managed through broken English to confide that she had never had a boyfriend. She seemed to have little life outside their home but declared herself to be quite content.

Emma's 15 year old brother, confusingly named Fernando, also lived there, running errands for them and generally living on whatever pocket money they could give him. He had a thick mop of black hair and bright, dark eyes that sparkled when he smiled. He was a bright lad who was universally popular but with sadly little hope of ever finding regular work. He was constantly torn between the relative comfort and security they gave him and moving to a larger town with better work prospects.

Another regular visitor to these dinner parties was an elderly black lady called Aura. She was 72, although she would variously tell people she was 82, 92 or, after a few glasses of port, 102. She had large liquid chocolate eyes that would (and did) charm the money from our pockets and the clothes from our backs. That is, until we got the measure of her.

Quite early on she had offered to store our possessions in her shed. She could, she assured us, look after any amount of food, crockery and boxes of any valuables we wished to keep safe; nothing was too much trouble.

Many of the things we managed to rescue from Salamander we, fortunately, kept with us, knowing they would soon be needed. We soon began to suspect and then to understand why our stock of tinned food was diminishing so quickly. In particular, we seemed to be getting through vast quantities of tinned spaghetti. We readily accepted there would be a cost for Aura's cooperation and wrote them off as a 'storage charge'.

Now, though, we had more space and had recovered what was left of our boxes from her shed. Back in the apartment we were able to make a more thorough inventory.

When we discovered that George's cut crystal whisky tumblers had disappeared along with a full set of cutlery, we were saddened and became uneasy over other items of value (sentimental or monetary) that we had left in her charge. The problem was remembering what we had put where.

Since we had moved to the apartment, Kim had spent several hours unsuccessfully searching for a favourite doll. No amount of rummaging through bags or boxes had relieved the anguish and we came to the unhappy conclusion that even some of the children's toys must have vanished in the same way. Resigned to causing no waves over Espinho's chosen way of doing things, we concluded this was simply part of the price we had to pay.

On one particularly rain sodden day, as we sat in Café Enfante, Aura arrived, clutching a bulging canvas bag. She sat quietly in the corner and the owner brought her a cup of black coffee. On his way back to the counter, he whispered the shocking news that there had been a fire at Aura's house. She lived in a tiny converted garage not much larger than the shed used to store our boxes. The fire had left large smoke marks throughout her kitchen-cum-living room. Knowing the misery of homelessness, Zoe and I immediately went to sit with her. Although she didn't understand English, we offered her all the sympathy we could and offered to inspect the damage and see if there was anything we could do to help. Miserably, she nodded and sipped her coffee.

Picking through the charred remains of her kitchen, it seemed the fire might have started somewhere near a worktop. The few electrical gadgets she owned were all apparently plugged into one overloaded socket, still swinging on the end of a now charred and melted cable attached to a light socket. The cause of the fire, at least, seemed pretty obvious.

I opened one of the cupboards. There, untouched by fire or smoke and stacked in neat rows without an inch to spare, were our tins of spaghetti. The next cupboard was the same and in the third, sitting patiently against a bottle of Heinz ketchup, was Kim's favourite doll.

We simply couldn't imagine the reason for taking a little girl's favourite toy. In total silence, we closed the doors and went back to the café.

Living with Aura was Donna Louise. Aura had taken her in some years earlier when she had nowhere to live. She was now 96 but never missed an opportunity for a night out at Café Enfante. John would tease her each time he left the café, asking whether he should go home now or, winking and nudging, 'take her home to tuck her up in bed.' On these occasions Donna Louise would defy her years, spring to her feet and bodily throw John out into the street. It must have been all that spaghetti that gave her the energy !

We should have expected these extraordinary contrasts of petty larceny and enormous generosity. At best, kindness was quite unlimited, especially as none of us had any idea when we would finally be able to leave and relieve them of their burden. Jorge's mother, for example, who we had not even met before she had offered us her apartment, invited Kim and Tania to join Jorge's youngest daughter Isabel and two other granddaughters, for a special children's dinner party. Even for a devoted grandmother, I reckoned that was service above and beyond the call of duty. It also allowed me and George to indulge ourselves with dinner in bed – prepared by Zoe. Such hedonistic luxury !!

The weekly routine Zoe and I had slipped into now also included visits to the local laundry. That is, the stream which ran through the middle of the village. Here, village housewives still took their dirty washing, along with a heavy bar of soap, and pounded their soaked clothes on the rocks. The rocks had been polished smooth by years of action by water and washer women while the water downstream was heavily polluted. It frothed with the dye from their clothes, carried in great tides of detergent scum along the banks of the stream.

There was always a struggle to get the position furthest up-stream and we soon learned this was wordlessly decided by the status of the household concerned. Surprisingly (and I think out of sympathy), we were allowed a relatively privileged position half way up the pecking order.

Their means of transporting large loads of laundry – and anything else – was quite simple. They twisted a small piece of cloth into a circle, put it on their heads, and placed the load to be carried on top.

After our visits to the laundry stream or the market, we often went out of our way to follow local housewives round the maze of side streets, taking whispered bets on whether any of the loads they carried would fall, or how it would be negotiated under the low doorways of their houses. It was quite usual for such interest to be sparked off by a dozen cardboard eggs trays or, on one notable occasion, a large polished grave stone that must have weighed over a hundredweight.

We regularly saw Fernander, effortlessly carrying a Calor Gas bottle on her head while holding two bags of shopping in each hand !

After returning from one such expedition, Zoe and I tried walking round the flat with an empty washing bowl on our heads. No matter how much we tried, it fell every time. The children thought it a wonderful game and, running to their bedroom to find suitable burdens to carry, quickly joined in. Returning home from a Salamandering session, George was more than a little bemused to find his family tangled in a heap on the tiled floor, along with plastic bowl, books and pillows, helpless with laughter.

On other occasions we went to the village roller-skating park and watched with admiration as adults and children alike skitted round the rink. Toddlers barely able to walk seemed perfectly at ease once mounted on wheels. Of course, Kim and Tania immediately decided they needed skates and George was persuaded to ask if we could borrow some in time for the next visit. There followed much excited discussion over the best techniques for speed skating, jumping and spinning through the air.

From time to time the rains held off long enough for us to spend a day at the beach or salvaging more from Salamander without getting totally saturated. During these brief spells working together, as the girls played happily along the sands, George, Zoe and I reflected on our future. Having spent our last reserves of cash on our, now redundant, tent, we were rapidly running out of rent money. It seemed more than likely that before very long we would find ourselves living under canvas after all. It wouldn't be the first time and when, sporadically and briefly, the sun shone we could treat the experience, for the children's sake at least, as a holiday. For these reasons we resisted any temptation to put our new camping equipment up for sale. Besides which, who in their right minds would buy a tent in this weather ??

OK, we did. But then we weren't in our right minds.

Any pleasure we might derive from warm weather would have to wait for many months. In the meantime, the downpour was relentless. It had been known to rain non-stop for six weeks at this time of year and we were more than grateful for the opportunity to stay in an apartment. We weren't sure why they didn't rent it out more often. It seemed such a waste when so many people were forced to live in broken down sheds and in houses held together and repaired with bits of old wood, corrugated metal or rough plaster. At that time of year, living in those conditions must have been as bad as camping.

We gained the impression that our landlords were wealthy enough not to need the extra income that regular tenants would have brought them and we knew we were paying well below the going rate. Few people in Espinho could have afforded to pay even that amount.

The miserable weather brought its lighter moments. We became accustomed to seeing mopeds and scooters buzzing along the sodden streets, entire families on board, huddled beneath an umbrella held against the wind by a pillion passenger. We spent lengthy conversations, killing time, speculating how a rogue gust of wind could scoop them up and carry the whole ensemble, Mary Poppins style, over the rooftops.

As each downpour began and we ran from one shelter to the next, splashing through deepening muddy puddles, we took any opportunity we could to visit one particular café close to Slamander's beach.

Possibly in our honour, a notice had appeared in the window shortly after our arrival. Written in blue crayon, it announced *'English we spoke here'*. The owner, as if nervous of false advertising laws, would always greet us by raising his hands to the ceiling and crying "Bye bye from myself," followed by an expectant smile. This, we invariably returned, with "Hola from ourselves", and a compliment on his English. After all, it was better than our Portuguese. I hope he didn't understand the sniggers from our little horrors, only partly suppressed behind their hands. Nevertheless, in common with most of Espinho's business community, he couldn't wait to slap George on the back and announce him to any who didn't already know that he was 'El Capitano'.

When, occasionally, we managed to sell a few clothes or bits of crockery we would celebrate with an English meal, usually thanks to Zoe's culinary skills. Large bowls of soup, steak, chips, peas, fried tomatoes and onion all chased down with wine, cheese and biscuits were invariably followed by days of remorse and strict dieting (for me and Zoe, at least). We constantly rebuked ourselves that we needed to lose at least a stone (all that Portuguese pasta !) and, will power not being our strong suit, were equally swift to promise, after a relapse, that a new diet would start tomorrow. It seldom did, but at least our habitual lack of cash prevented us from bingeing on cream cakes and chocolate.

Every attempt to diet was a lost cause before it started. Whichever café we visited, following an inevitable "Hola Capitano" we would, without asking or being asked, be indulged with heavy slices of cake and large mugs of steaming hot chocolate.

At the beginning of November, almost two months after being unceremoniously dumped in Espinho, we managed to get our passports stamped. The authorities now officially, and somewhat reluctantly, acknowledged that we were in Portugal.

They were always quicker over the business of collecting their revenue. Within days of selling anything, we were summoned to Porto to pay duty and taxes. The first time this had happened, the bill had been £300. When George later did some calculations, he worked out they had left us a balance of just under £100.

Trying to raise the necessary cash to buy a car was proving an even steeper climb than we had thought. The longer we stayed, the more we needed to keep ourselves and the more we had to sell. The more we had to sell, the more we had to pay in tax. The longer this took, the less we had left to buy a car and therefore the longer we had to stay... Would the cycle ever end ?

We then heard that the Spanish border with Gibraltar had been closed. Stories were filtering off The Rock that unemployment was spiralling as a result of the sudden drop in trade with Spain. One of our hopes had been that, if we were able to get there, we could have earned enough to fund our onward journey. Now, even that option seemed to have been taken away.

Nevertheless, we wrote to the Gibraltar Tourist Information Office enquiring about crossing the border from Spain and finding temporary accommodation. We mentioned nothing of our intention to look for jobs, rather hoping our letter gave the impression of reasonably wealthy Brits in search of an English education for their daughters.

We had long before given up any possibility of finding work in Espinho. There was no work and we had no work permits. We also felt we needed to find somewhere warmer. Gibraltar had seemed ideal, especially as there would be no language barrier.

We were never to receive a reply. Perhaps they saw through our ploy or, just as likely, the local postal service let us down. We will never know.

Having time on my hands I constantly found myself reflecting on our situation in a most impractical way. Our early 'what if' dreams that had driven us south to Espinho had turned somewhat maudlin. Zoe's cheerful optimism and philosophical answer that we were learning by our experiences kept us going through the blacker moments, while Kim and Tania both simply accepted everything fate threw at them as being perfectly normal.

I couldn't help noticing, though, how my solid, unshakeable and dependable George had been affected. Although he did his best to hide it, his pride and self-confidence had been hit harder than any of us knew.

When John and Paula had dropped out before we had even started, he had accepted their decision as part of the process of natural selection. Without total commitment, any member of the team would have become a liability. He had said at the time, it was far better they didn't come with us at all than to drop out half way round Europe. George had quickly adapted, nobody felt any ill effects, and our plans and suffered no great problems as a result.

When Colin, Barbara and Steve had left, though, he had been deeply upset and felt personally let down. He hadn't understood then how they could have chosen to leave and now, weeks later, still didn't believe their reasons were good enough. He had felt a great respect for Colin in particular, and that made their decision all the more difficult to take.

Nevertheless, at the time, he had accepted their departure without argument and had put up a good pretence that it didn't matter. In our quieter moments, we wondered aloud whether, with an extra three crew members on board, we would have been beached. Such depressing thoughts did nothing to help us resolve our problems and were dismissed as hastily as possible. These quiet discussions and private thoughts we preferred not to share with Zoe. I was determined that her rays of sunny optimism would not be blackened by such recriminations.

To add insult to injury, we heard rumours from home that Steve was complaining he had lost money on the trip. His only contribution had been £100 towards food and diesel and, as Zoe pointed out, somewhat sheepishly, she had lent him money towards his living expenses. She doubted that it would be repaid and hadn't attempted to contact him about it since our arrival in Espinho. She knew how useful extra cash would have been, but equally knew the futility of such a request.

George sniffed. "We'll manage. It'll be all right. You'll see."

As a means of cheering himself up and proving that we had a future worth working towards, multi-talented George announced his decision to start up in business in Guernsey as a masseur – something he had proved he had an aptitude for, in addition to his skills as maritime navigator and engineer. He had already been offered two such jobs in Espinho but had felt he had to decline.

He reasoned that his earnings would have to be balanced against the lost Salamandering time. Apart from that, the risk of being caught by the authorities loomed large. In such a small town everyone would soon know what we were up to and, needless to say in an area of high unemployment, the authorities would take a dim view of anyone found working without the required permit. A permit, John and Jorge both assured us, which even if we bothered to apply for, would be refused.

Instead, we were invited to become honorary members of the local athletics club. In exchange for the use of their facilities and countless (and technically illegal) payments of food and provisions, George became their physiotherapist. It wasn't long before he was also tending to the muscular needs of the Roller Hockey team and we were in danger of becoming accepted as part of the local furniture.

Nevertheless, this boost to his flagging ego and decision to take up the work professionally at home seemed to revitalise his spirits. A new start would give us an opportunity to recover the £25,000 we had just lost. It had taken us just four weeks to lose it and, to George, his challenge was to see how quickly he could regain it.

Meanwhile, the only thing that seemed to upset Kim were her growing pains which, like most six year olds, took the form of momentous tantrums. I have never approved of smacking children and found very early in my parenting career that shouting does absolutely no good at all. She could invariably out-shout me and her endurance was phenomenal.

Instead, the withdrawal of a treat carried the most weight. The difficulty, during these Spartan times, was in finding a treat to withhold. One of her more spectacular tantrums led to her being grounded while the rest of us visited John and

Fernander. Zoe selflessly offered to stay and baby-sit, which left me with double the normal level of guilt and doubt as we left the flat.

It was supposed to be Kim's punishment but, as the door closed, we heard her wail crescendo into a full scale bellow of outrage. It crossed my mind that it was Zoe who was actually suffering the punishment.

I waited a few seconds before surreptitiously opening the front door again. Kim was lying, red faced, on the floor, damp eyes and fists clenched, pounding and kicking the tiles. She didn't notice me, concentrating as she was on making the loudest possible noise without drawing breath.

Zoe was sitting calmly next to her. She nodded at me reassuringly, mouthing "I can cope" and waving me away.

We returned at 10 pm to find the apartment in serene silence. Kim didn't even look up as we entered, seated on the sofa next to Zoe with her feet curled up beneath her. Her expression one of ecstasy, as if she had undergone a deeply spiritual transformation, she purred that Zoe had been teaching her to knit.

This was to become an activity preferable to any treat we could dream up and taught her more about self sufficiency and concentration than we could ever have taught her. So much for punishment !

Kim's education, although unconventional, was going well. Her self-confidence was building steadily and she was learning how to do simple sums, although her reading was well below the standard we would have liked. This was hardly surprising, bearing in mind that all the children's books, brought with us with the best possible intentions, had been rendered useless by sea water and rain.

Tania had also changed but, unlike Kim, was showing no indication of growing into a lady – apart from a natural preference for the company of men. I have to admit she was showing signs of becoming spoiled and could, with no effort whatsoever, completely dominate both Kim and George. Any precocious behaviour she might have displayed had been made all the greater by her pride at learning to swim and ride a bike.

As far as she was concerned, however, her greatest achievements remained the production of new teeth, which were now beginning to appear almost daily. Several times a day, I would find her carefully inspecting her open mouth in the mirror, feeling around her gums with an exploratory finger for evidence of new arrivals.

Just one week after having our passports stamped and our entry and presence in Portugal declared official, we discovered we had once again become illegal immigrants. The temporary visas we had been issued expired on 7th November.

The sky didn't come crashing in on us. Neither did the immigration authorities. It had taken them several weeks to acknowledge our existence, so now that we were illegal again, we hoped it would take them another few weeks to catch up.

As George reasoned, what was the worst thing they could do ? Deport us ?

Instead of chasing round after immigration officials and their rubber stamps, we continued in our endeavours to find a way out of our impasse by meeting with Saint Jorge and anyone he could muster who might, in one way or another, be able to help. There was a rumour going about that a local man was trying to sell a Citroen van. It was older than the Opel Rekord, but we had long since agreed that every opportunity was worth exploring. This was particularly true when it came to getting ourselves a vehicle, as the owner of the Opel had made no promises that he would keep it for us if another buyer came along. Bearing in mind our current financial situation, we could hardly blame him.

Spurred on by yet more rumours that someone was interested in buying our generator, George and Zoe went to inspect the van. It was a large and extremely battered eleven year old with corrugated side panels and a 'for sale' sign written in Portuguese in the window. They slowly circled the vehicle, debating how many miles it had left in it and studying various dents and a front wing that seemed to be parting company from the bonnet.

It would, at least, have been large enough to carry everything from Salamander, saving us much effort and time – and therefore money. The price we could get for our possessions would be far greater in Guernsey and we would be free of tax problems. George was far too practical to get carried away with the prospect without fully examining all the angles. The obvious down side was that, with or without a boat full of bric-a-brac, the van would have little room for passengers. As he and Zoe were prodding at a particularly rust covered corner, the owner appeared.

He stood, despite the chill weather, in dirty dark blue trousers and sweaty singlet, a damp home-rolled cigarette stuck thinly to his lower lip. He folded his arms, weighing up the pair circling his van.

George feigned disinterest, drawing his breath in doubtfully before asking how much he wanted for it.

The answer, quickly converted into sterling, amounted to a little over £3,000. Zoe exhaled suddenly, making raspberry noises. George, showing great restraint, simply shook his head. He told him, as courteously as he could in very broken Portuguese, that he must be mad. He offered him £500. The owner waved them away dismissively, turned on his heel and sauntered back into his house.

Another ambition shattered. We were clearly not destined to become the proud owners of a Citroen van of dubious pedigree and expired sell-by date.

That brief episode seemed to signal another downward slide. Eleven days after becoming illegal immigrants again, Kim and Tania finally showing signs of home-sickness, we learned that if we left Portugal before satisfying all governmental demands, we would lose all rights to our possessions and the proceeds from any sales.

In other words, if we couldn't get Salamander off the beach, or we failed to pay any of the tax they were demanding, we would lose the right to take home anything we had not sold. We would also have to hand over all the money we had received from the things we had sold plus the tax.

As Salamander had clearly put down roots and the tax demand already exceeded the value of the goods, this latest bit of news merely served to convince us we really were in Wonderland. All we needed now was a white rabbit insisting he was late, and the image would have been complete.

To try and cheer us up, Saint Jorge resorted to a traditional Portuguese remedy. He invited us for a meal. Despite my hesitation, following George's experience of Jorge's strange taste in cuisine, we were served with a wonderful meal. The plates were delicate English porcelain, the cutlery solid silver. We sat at a heavily carved oak dining table on eight impressive matching leather upholstered chairs, somewhat uneasily watching the girls and the pristine white linen table cloth before them.

Against one wall and dominating the room stood a fine carved oak dresser with a stuffed vulture perched on top of it. Its wings half extended as if to take flight, I couldn't help but feel the glass eyes were following my every mouthful.

Traditional potato soup and watercress were followed by tender pieces of roast pork, served with slices of lightly grilled tomato and a huge tureen of baked potatoes. We barely had room for the final courses of cream gateaux, hot chestnuts in wine sauce, followed by port and brandy.

We were left, once more, humbled by their generosity and good will, amazed at the contrasts of this little town and quite unable to move.

A steady trickle of prospective buyers for our salvage had filtered our way, via Jorge and Café Enfante. Most had lost interest as soon as they learned how much tax the Government would want but slowly, a few Escudos at a time, we managed to gather together £300. On 25th November, hearts fluttering, we paid this over as a deposit on the Opel Rekord and a two wheeled aluminium trailer. As George sagely commented, he would do any reversing needed. It wasn't that I couldn't reverse with a trailer. We had dragged enough caravans around Europe for me to become quite practised. I just had this irritating habit of forgetting it was there, especially while trying to find a space in supermarket car parks. Despite sleeping on a cold wet boat and an equally cold and wet floor, I didn't think I could face any nights in Portuguese or Spanish police cells.

We were feeling more than a little imprisoned as it was. The daily grind of trying to find buyers, of ways to get the generator and engine out of Salamander, of sorting through surplus clothes and of fighting bureaucracy without any prospect of work or wages were getting to all of us. We alleviated the boredom a little by teaching ourselves a new Portuguese word each day.

The day we paid the deposit on the Opel, our word was 'snuba'. It means 'rain'.

We hoped we wouldn't have to learn the Portuguese for sleet, hail or snow and equally hoped we would be away before Christmas. This hope became a fervent promise to ourselves when we realised that, with just four weeks to go, there were no festive decorations in the shops. We were told Christmas was just like any other public holiday. Everybody expected to be back to their normal routine by Boxing Day. It didn't sound like the sort of Christmas we were used to !

I have to admit to a little bit of pre-festive season depression, having no spare money to buy Christmas presents for Zoe or the girls. George soon set me straight. As usual, his philosophy and wisdom were both simple and honest. Those things that we couldn't do anything about, we should waste no time trying to change. Instead we should make the best of them and use our energies improving those things we could change.

November turned to December and Porto's Fire Brigade expressed an interest in buying Salamander's water pump. At last, a buyer that, we presumed, had some money. In addition, the Chief of Police, who had taken over the duties of tax collector, had promised to visit us and discuss ways of reducing our tax bill. We were sure Saint Jorge had been at work behind the scenes again, pulling strings or, at least, calling in outstanding favours on our behalf.

The Police Chief, however, failed to turn up on the appointed Wednesday although we waited in all day for him. A message arrived, written in English on a piece of headed notepaper, asking us to 'phone him the following day. Finally the meeting took place on the following Saturday.

Our discussion, via a police interpreter, was never less than courteous and we remained attentive to all he was telling us. Zoe ferried in relays of coffee and cakes and George took notes of salient points, keen to show we took the situation seriously.

After nearly three hours, finally, the officer placed both his hands, palms down, on the low table between us. He shrugged slightly as he spoke, his eyes now lowered to inspect his fingernails.

The interpreter, who had throughout the lengthy debate expressed no emotion whatever as he translated, told us in his monotone that there could, after consideration, be no further concession.

What concession, George politely enquired, had we thus far been given ?

"The officer has permitted you to keep various items of property without tax."

George looked puzzled. "Did I miss something ? What items ?"

Prompted by the Police Chief, the interpreter consulted a list. "Items of clothing. Food. Personal belongings ..."

I could see George's jaw tightening. "The officer will forgive me if we are not completely overwhelmed with gratitude."

The interpreter spoke in emotionless Portuguese while the officer shuffled slightly in his seat and mumbled a reply.

"The officer asks if this is English humour."

"No," replied George. "If it were humour, it would be funny." He paused, waiting for his words to sink in. There was no reaction.

I asked whether, had we been tourists taking a package holiday in Espinho, we would have been required to pay tax on the clothes in our suitcases.

Again the policeman and interpreter conferred. The latter shrugged. "Of course not. There are no tourists in Espinho."

"I wonder why."

Despite the professed generosity of our host nation's officials, we were by now running extremely low on food. Our tins, or those left us by Aura, at least, were fast running out. In some ways, I was relieved that our monotonous diet of tinned spaghetti and beans was nearly at an end. Although we couldn't have managed without them, I resolved not to open another tin for at least six months after we got back to Guernsey.

George had explained during our meeting that, in our efforts to raise the cash we needed, we had reduced the asking price of the generator from £5,000 to £3,500. Now, with a bill for £1,900 for tax on that one item, we had dropped the price again to £2,500. Similarly, the compressor had been reduced to £1,050 of which £900 would have to be paid in tax.

Despite the despotic rate of taxation, if we managed to sell both of them we would be well on our way to paying for the car and moving on.

Any other money we managed to make was, by then, going on fresh fruit and vegetables for the children and, despite the gifts given to us for George's work at the hockey and sports clubs, we were still having to dip into our diminishing cash reserve to make ends meet.

It was extraordinary how the children had been persuaded that a meal of bacon and boiled cabbage which at home they wouldn't touch without the bribe of an ice cream, had now become a weekly treat.

It was at about this time that I started getting nightmares. They were always the same; the morning of September 7th, the seas heavy with foam and oil, thick fog choking us, Salamander running aground, her old hull splintering, the deck falling away beneath us. We fall uncontrollably and the timbers seem to devour us, opening and closing above us like giant jaws. The jagged edges of the decking become sharp rotten teeth, tearing at us as we tumble towards the engulfing oil. I reach out, trying to grab Kim's T-shirt. My fingers close round the thin fabric, but it falls apart between my fingers and Kim's tiny arms and legs flail helplessly. Finally, falling, she twists round to face me but instead of her round cherubic face, there is Lucifer, telling me to eat all ... eat all. He laughs demonically and I wake, damp with cold sweat, heart pounding and the vision of £25,000 all in pound notes running away on the tide.

I tried not to wake George whenever this happened. He had his own demons to fight. He was already feeling guilty enough about what we were going through. Instead, I would sit in the darkness, pinching my arms and forcing myself to shake off any thoughts of lost money or possessions. What did cash matter when we had all survived. I still had my wonderful husband and daughters. Zoe was still with us, helping us to fight back. How different things might have been. The thought echoed around my head of having to explain to my mum that I had lost her granddaughters – or to Zoe's mum that her daughter wouldn't be coming home.

We had a lot to be thankful for.

The day after one of these nightmares, George told me how he had seen a young girl sitting by the side of the road not far from our apartment. She had been dressed very shabbily with no shoes and had been clutching a sickly baby of a few months old. He had given them his last few Escudos. It only amounted to around ten pence, but it was all he had in his pocket.

George's story was disturbing enough for me to substitute it for the memory of my nightmare and provided an answer to George's intuitive question of why I seemed upset. Zoe's normal bright expression had deepened to a frown. We both knew we were thinking of the same thing. Together, we packed a bag with clothes – the sizes judged from George's descriptions, along with some food and headed off to look for them.

They were exactly where George had last seen them. The girl was about eleven years old. She had a small round face and could have modelled as an East End urchin for an illustration in a Dickens novel. Large brown bush-baby eyes followed us as we approached. We smiled encouragingly but got no response. She made no move when we put the bag down next to her, gesturing for her to take it. Eventually, she peered inside, smiled shyly and tucked it away behind her.

The following day she was back in the same place again, dressed in the same torn and grubby clothes, despite those we had given her being in far better condition. We guessed that with her pretty looks and small infant brother, by dividing her time carefully between each of the local towns and villages, she was making as good a living as any in Espinho.

She was almost certainly doing better than we were. I had already told Tania and Kim, in as casual and cheerful way as I could, that we would have Christmas late this year. They had looked at me suspiciously and immediately wished to know how late, and why, and had Father Christmas said so ?

Christmas would be in about May because, I improvised, Father Christmas would find it too difficult to bring their presents all the way to Portugal.

They had always been very good about toys, putting up with our rationing when we left Guernsey and then even stricter reductions after we lost Salamander. They now had one precious teddy bear each and a few remaining books – which they were far less impressed with.

In an effort to provide ourselves with some reading material of our own, we tried exchanging two of our books for one new one at a local shop that kept a few English language novels. These precious imports normally sold for three times the price of Portuguese books and the shop owner wasn't interested in trading.

Thanks to John's taste in reading material, the paperbacks that George had managed to save from the elements and the lack of anything else to do during the evenings, I had managed to get through a rich variety of books that normally I wouldn't have even glanced at.

I was now an expert on the Bermuda Triangle, marine salvage and the novels of Rider Haggart.

We didn't manage to leave Espinho by Christmas. When *'The Press'* (our Guernsey newspaper) arrived on Christmas Eve, thoughtfully sent out to us by friends, George and I fought over who would read it first and avidly absorbed every word. Along with a long gossipy letter from one of our neighbours, it was the best Christmas present I could have hoped for. I felt quite ashamed that, when at home, I had barely bothered to keep up with local affairs but used the newspapers more to check when my favourite soap operas were going to be on. Pointlessly, I looked down the TV listings and wondered how the residents of Coronation Street and Albert Square were getting on without me. Such had been the intensity of our preparations before leaving home that I had barely seen any television since the previous summer.

In another effort to get a little extra money, we returned one of our two Calor Gas bottles to the local supplier and had our deposit returned. We now ate few hot meals and washed in cold water to cut down our fuel consumption. We just had to hope the next few Escudos would arrive before the gas ran out. I sorted through our remaining tins for the umpteenth time, searching for foods which could be served cold. I didn't fancy cold baked beans or processed peas. I wondered how long we could survive on cold rice pudding.

As George pointed out, we could have tried fishing for our supper, but the sea was so rough and the stream so polluted with detergents, the effort would have been wasted.

I managed to sell my faithful old sewing machine. It was one of the last possessions we had left and the cash from the sale kept us well fed for over a week. By that time we had just one week remaining in our apartment, based on the rent money we had paid in advance to Jorge's parents. Once the week was up, unless we had raised the cash to pay the final instalment on the car, we would have no option but to move, rain or no rain, onto the camp site.

Despite the weather, which we would have thought of as being both miserable and disastrous at home, the local rivers, we were assured, were lower than normal for that time of year. The farmers were praying in earnest for more rain to feed their crops. According to Jorge, they needed the downpour to continue for at least another month to restore their supplies and keep them through the spring and summer. If our luck ran true to form and Mother Nature continued her campaign of attrition against us, their prayers would surely be answered.

We had lived under canvas in wet conditions before, but had experienced nothing to compare with winter on the Portuguese Atlantic coast. George and I have never sought a luxurious life-style and had always believed that the girls should be brought up to expect a little hardship from time to time. If nothing else, we were fulfilling that ambition.

Christmas having been postponed, it was difficult to explain to the girls how it was that we wouldn't be able to visit John and Fernander for a while as they had gone to England to visit his family over the festive season. That was disappointing enough, but another bombshell had just been primed and was about to drop.

While on a mission in Porto to sell some of our marine parts and George's tools, Jorge's car was stolen. He had only bought it a few days before and all the car's documents, including his driving licence and several receipts for the tax we had already paid had all been in the glove compartment. The tools, three children's life jackets, a marine radio set and a bilge pump had all been in the boot.

Also in the car had been our certificate, stamped and signed by officials after much negotiation and argument, that the tax payable on the generator had been agreed.

According to Jorge, unless the Ministry officials were in a generous mood and provided us with a duplicate, we might have to start the negotiations all over again. This was a question which would go unanswered for several weeks. Despite the public holiday lasting only a day or two, the civil servants' working pace had now slowed to a laboured crawl until well into the New Year.

Having arrived home from Porto in a taxi and delivered the news, Jorge readily conceded that the police were most unlikely to recover his car. That was part of the reason for the high cost of motor insurance. He would add the value of our lost possessions to his claim but, he admitted, settlement might well take several months.

As some sort of compensation, we were all invited to Café Enfante on Christmas Eve to drown our collective sorrows and consider our strategy in case the bureaucrats ganged up on us again.

When we arrived, the doors were locked and the blinds firmly pulled down. We were amazed to find that we were being invited to join them for their family celebration. And what a family ! There were aunts, uncles, grandparents, nieces, nephews and cousins of every description. The little café was fuller than we had ever seen it. We were ushered in and warmly welcomed, shaken by the hand, introduced and kissed at least twice by each and every one of them. Glasses of port were immediately offered and gladly accepted. A toast was offered in Portuguese, instantly translated as a welcome to their friends from abroad. We drank. We chatted in a broken mixture of English, Spanish, Portuguese and French. We laughed. We relaxed for the first time in days and we were grateful.

Their traditional festive meal consisted of fish that had been hung up during the previous Christmas holiday. Having dried out for a full twelve months it was now served raw and shredded with onions and vinegar. Laughing at the little horrors' wrinkled noses and our, hopefully less obvious, hesitation, they produced a wonderful meal of rich soup with wine, followed by grilled chicken, roast potatoes, peas and kale in delicious rich sauce. Kim being instantly suspicious, even after so long, of any food not immediately identifiable and familiar, we managed to convince her that kale was cabbage and the sauce was gravy.

As side dishes, they prepared slices of fresh bread, soaked in port and brushed with beaten egg before being baked in the oven.

Bearing in mind we had just a few hours earlier resigned ourselves to tinned spaghetti and mushy peas (which represented all we had left of our tins) the meal was a truly spectacular success.

I thought the girls were going to burst with excitement (and over indulgence) when they saw a large tray being brought in piled high with light fluffy doughnuts, a large jug of rich, thick custard and a vast triple layered chocolate gateau.

How we would ever equal this next Christmas I couldn't imagine and just hoped the little horrors didn't expect a repeat performance at the postponed Christmas we had promised for May.

All this was followed by small cups of thick strong coffee – the thicker and stronger the better, apparently, as it acted as a stimulant and allowed celebrations to continue long into the night. Regrettably, it had the desired effect on George.

He decided that, to repay their hospitality, it would be only fair to provide some traditional English entertainment. After a large glass of port, he called for silence and, clearing his throat, gave a passable rendition of 'Once in Royal David's City'. Another large port and we were rewarded with the first verse of 'Away in a Manger'. A third, even larger glass and 'Good King Wenceslas' sounded more like a Bavarian drinking song.

Zoe and I had already shrunk into a quiet corner and were debating ways that we could disown him when, to my horror, I heard the strains of 'Sarnia Cheri – Gem of the Sea'. Always one of George's favourites, it was only ever given an airing when he was in a particularly mellow frame of mind. My hands covered my face and, during a pause between verses, I risked a glance from between my fingers. Zoe's smiling face blinked back. Well, she reasoned, if a husband can't embarrass his wife on Christmas eve, when can he embarrass her?

I calculated that I still had plenty of time to get my own back and was just deciding how, when I realised the warbling tones were no longer delivering a solo. The rest of the guests were joining in. Those who didn't know the words, hummed along while others conducted the chorus with batons of spoons and forks.

Before long, the tables and chairs in the little café had been pushed to the edges of the room. Two guitars were produced and expertly played by two of the café owner's four sons, the eldest son providing the rhythm with a pair of drums, giving evidence to his claim of being a professional drummer.

He played in a pop group but, apparently, would have far preferred to spend his evenings playing 'In The Mood' or 'Chatanooga Choo-Choo' with a big band. As his uncle explained, there weren't many big bands around any more and, in any case, girls were far more impressed by a pop star.

While another nephew joined in with a piano accordion, the owner himself showed he was the possessor of a fine and powerful tenor voice and his brother a mean ukulele player. They took it in turns to choose their favourite pieces of music, each musician seeming to know the full family repertoire.

Those who couldn't play, sang and danced. Kim and Tania were included throughout, dancing with each of the young nephews and cousins in turn.

It is difficult to imagine our own teenagers being so generous with their attention or so lacking in self consciousness that they would happily spend time entertaining young children. Here, it seemed to be second nature, spontaneous and totally genuine. At the same time, young and old happily consumed large quantities of drink without any signs of drunkenness or misbehaviour.

The party continued, the joy and bonhomie unrelenting, until four o'clock in the morning. We got home just as the earliest strands of sunlight appeared between the mountains and the first birds of the day began testing their voices.

Surprisingly – although it was Christmas Day – the little horrors woke and were trampling around the apartment at their usual ungodly hour of the morning. We had managed just under four hours sleep, but that didn't dissuade them that the day needed to be enjoyed to the full.

We had scraped together enough Escudos to spend about £1 on each of them and had put small presents in a sock at the foot of their beds. Bleary eyed, George and I watched with growing misgivings as they opened their tiny parcels and lined up their gifts in front of them. Each had a piece of fruit, a small bag of sweets and a tiny doll in Portuguese national costume. We were so glad they were of an age to accept our changing fortunes without question and thankful that they weren't surrounded by children being buried under all the latest games and toys.

Our Christmas lunch consisted of ham rolls, a bottle of port and Portuguese style Christmas cake; a circular loaf of heavy bread, decorated with glazed fruit.

We sat in the kitchen, having eaten the last crumb, taunting each other with the imagined meals being enjoyed by our friends and families at home. Roast turkey, stuffing, little sausages with bacon wrapped round them, mince pies...

Within days we were soberly returned to our state of melancholy by the news that the buyer for our generator had pulled out. The £600 we had agreed was no problem, but he couldn't afford the tax. Truth be told, even if we had offered to give him the damn thing, he still wouldn't have been able to accept it as the tax the Government placed on it was based on their own wholly unrealistic estimate of its value.

Saint Jorge had tried to persuade them that the generator and the other equipment were all worth far less than they estimated. The proof of our argument being that nobody would consider buying them at the values they placed on them.

The bureaucrats' replies to this varied, depending on who he spoke to. One official said they based their valuation on an engineer's report (the fee for which, incidentally, was added to the tax bill). Another said it was based on the cost of a similar piece of equipment, bought brand new, minus an amount for depreciation calculated by some impossible formula using the age of the salvaged equipment and distance Salamander's log showed she had travelled. Because Salamander's documentation had been lost, we had no proof of either figure and their reckoning was based on guesswork. We never established what those guesses might have been, but they clearly chose not to believe she had been built as long ago as the last war. A third official told us confidently that their valuation was all based on weight!

It was now Zoe's turn to become depressed. To be fair, she probably had more reason than any of us to feel the strain. Not only was she a teenager, stranded away from home with no friends of her own age to mix with. She had even less control over our situation than we did.

As she had said on several occasions, had we been stranded in Torremolinos or Marbella – or any other holiday resort, she could easily have got work in a bar and contributed to the money we needed. As it was, she professed to feeling totally useless. I did my best to convince her otherwise.

In truth, had we been in a holiday resort our outlook would have been entirely different. We would have blended in far easier and would all have been able to work unnoticed. On the other hand, we would have had to pay much more for our accommodation. It is also likely that the local people would have been far less sympathetic and generous. Without Zoe's sunny outlook, I promised her, I would have gone mad and the children would have been miserable. She had done more than could possibly have been expected of her. I meant every word, but her mood seemed, for once, to be immovably low. However inadequate, the only short-term remedy I could think of was the offer of a few drinks at a nearby bar. It did nothing to raise her spirits and she simply shook her head and gazed at the floor.

She was long overdue some peace and quiet and a rest from us all. I told her where we would be if she changed her mind. George and I quietly gathered the girls together and slipped out of the flat. I had never seen Zoe looking so deflated. We had become so used to her smiling all the time, it was easy to forget she might be homesick and subject to the same disappointments we were going through.

Being terminally short of money, we decided to take a stroll out of the village before returning to the bar. We were entertained along the way by a vivid example of Portuguese highway etiquette.

We were approaching a deep river valley, along the bottom of which flowed one of the tributaries from the River Douro. On each side of this steep gorge, snaked the only road between Espinho and Porto. As we walked we could see and hear two lorries approaching from opposite directions. One, a giant eight wheeled monster, the other a small articulated wagon, hauled by a three wheeled covered tractor.

Between them lay a long single lane bridge spanning the valley and only wide enough for one vehicle to cross at a time. As they closed on each other from either side of the river, they both accelerated, equally determined to cross first and in clear view of each other across the void.

At the last moment, a few yards from the centre of the bridge, they simultaneously slammed on their brakes. They came to rest in the centre, surrounded by clouds of dust and black diesel fumes, no more than two feet separating their front bumpers.

Neither moved. Like great forest beasts, testing the other's determination, they revved their engines and pushed down on their horns, bellowing in indignation. The larger of the two uttered a deep, growling roar, while the smaller three-wheeler whinnied like a shire horse.

Finally, both drivers climbed out of their cabs. Emerging from the small cab above the three wheels, a huge man in crumpled grey flannel trousers and collarless shirt unfolded himself, standing over his vehicle and pulling at his braces before approaching his opponent.

Climbing down from his giant cab using the front wheel as an additional step, the second driver, eight stone of whippet-like sinew, pulled himself up to his full five feet. In the shadow of his wagon, he straightened his outsized cap and marched purposefully forward. They met between the bumpers. The larger man bent down, their noses inches apart.

George and I were transfixed. "Fred Flintstone meets Norman Wisdom." Glancing down at the girls, we were thankful that their argument, conducted at full volume and echoing off the valley walls, was in incomprehensible Portuguese. The small man, turning red with rage, tore the cap from his head and hurled it to the ground.

The larger man, smiling a gap tooth grin, stamped his heel down and ground it into the sludge that was a permanent winter feature.

The red face turned an even darker hue as the owner of the cap clenched his little fists in front of his chin, jumping up and down like a music hall comic performing an exaggerated shadow boxing routine.

By now, a growing line of other vehicles had built up behind each lorry. Motorists were lazily sticking their heads out of their windows or leaning on doors to watch the drama unfold at the head of their queue. Only those who couldn't get a proper view sounded their horns. A youngster on a moped wove a complex path between the stationary vehicles to get closer to the action.

At the back of one of the queues the driver of a Citroen Deux Chevaux had rolled back the car's canvas roof and lifted himself up to sit on the back of the driver's seat. He leaned forward, resting his elbows on the top of the windscreen. He settled down to enjoy the view over the traffic jam, tapping the horn from time to time with his foot.

Now, even if either of the lorry drivers had wished to concede, the task would have involved a perplexing array of shunting, reversing and three point turns from the string of cars behind them.

The argument, fuelled on each side by supportive gestures and shouts of encouragement from the motorists held in the traffic jam, rose to fever pitch.

The smaller man was almost beside himself with rage, jumping up on the bumper of his lorry to gain extra height. Despite trying the manoeuvre three times, he fell off on each occasion, only causing the other driver to mock him all the more, slapping his heavy thigh and holding his shaking stomach in exaggerated mirth.

After some ten minutes of this, the big man seemed to lose his sense of humour. He swiped the air with a careless backhand above the other's head and sat back on the bonnet of his truck, arms folded. When the other failed to move, and apparently tiring of the game, he stood upright again, his chest inches from the smaller driver's upturned face. He spat on his great hands and, with slow deliberation, rolled up his sleeves. A sudden stillness descended over the bridge. The car horns fell silent and urgent hushing noises told the drivers behind that something was about to happen that demanded their attention.

The big man took a pace forward, looked down briefly at the other driver, then stepped deliberately past him. He squatted down, bending at the knees and wrapped his thick arms round a massive boulder lying by the side of the road.

He took two quick gulps of air and in a sudden and surprisingly graceful movement lifted it in a wide arc and lofted it over the railing at the side of the bridge.

He didn't wait to see it fall but turned and walked back to his cab. He crouched into it and the engine fired up again. He reversed a foot or so, pulled the wheel hard over and, scraping the side of his wagon down the metal railings of the bridge and tearing both wing mirrors from their mountings, forced his wagon past the other lorry over the spot where the boulder had been.

A loud cheer erupted along both sides of the bridge and immediately a string of smaller vehicles started moving forward in the wake of their leader. Belittled, the diminutive driver examined his mudguard, dented and minus its wing mirror. He picked up his cap from the mud, realised it had just been run over and threw it angrily over the side.

The drama resolved, we continued our stroll, shortly being passed by a donkey pulling a small open cart. The dark haired gypsy at the reigns, oblivious to the line of traffic crawling along behind them, was dressed in traditional style; smartly sombre dark grey suit and outrageously contrasting bright red and orange shirt. Beside him his wife, in a full skirt, colourful blouse and large gold hoop earrings, carried a small child in a shawl wrapped round her shoulders. She leaned back against a pile of furniture, tea chests and a metal dustbin on which perched two small children of about the same ages as Kim and Tania.

Roped behind the cart another donkey plodded patiently along, ridden bareback by a boy of about eight. Paying no attention to the road or his surroundings, he swung a yo-yo up and down with casual expertise.

"All their worldly goods ?" mused George, more to himself than anyone else.

There was silence for a few moments. "It's a thought, isn't it ?" I asked.

"What is ?"

I jerked my thumb over my shoulder at the departing cart. "Do you think it would get us to St.Malo ?"

George gazed at me in a way which could possibly have meant 'Don't be daft'. On the other hand, it might have meant 'It may not be so daft. I won't rule it out'. There are times when George can be infuriatingly inscrutable.

We had seen families like this at the market. The Gypsies seemed to have been allocated their own section to set up their stalls and from which they sold anything from pegs to ponies. They bartered with anything that had any value. They always came prepared with several wooden boxes to take away any chickens or other small livestock acquired during the day's trading. Despite that, the aprons they tied round themselves on market days were invariably stuffed with tens of thousands of Escudos.

During these market days, the men would sit back, dozing in deckchairs or on their carts while their womenfolk did the haggling. Nobody seemed to look after the children who, in any case, were easy to pick out in the crowd by their dark skin and jet black hair.

We were delighted to be invited again to Café Enfante for New Year's Eve. The language difference, as ever, proved to be no barrier at all and we stayed until 4 am. At home, the disapproving looks of sour faced parents would have driven us home hours earlier. Those were the parents who left their children in the care of baby-sitters, with instructions on matters such as their offspring's designated bed-time, snacks, TV shows, video games and bed time stories. They were the same parents who, at the first hint of mistreatment, would have rushed to their 'phones to call Social Services, the NSPCC or Esther Rantzen. Put another way, they were parents like us. Perhaps we were just 'going native'.

Much fun was had by all and, to her enormous and almost indiscreetly obvious delight, Zoe was invited out on a date by Ismael. He was tall, dark, decidedly good looking and had kept up an uninterrupted line in whispered small-talk, close to Zoe's ear, since the moment he was introduced to her. He was also a sports star, being the goalkeeper for the local Roller Hockey team and the son of a wealthy local industrialist.

The following Saturday evening we all visited the roller skating rink. It had become a weekly treat for the girls, especially since Ismael, now an inseparable friend, had been going out of his way to teach them how to stay on their feet.

Was it, we wondered, his way of gaining Zoe's favour ? George and I concluded it wasn't. He seemed a genuinely nice young man and, like most of the local people of his age we had met so far, chivalrous and old fashioned in his attitudes. Anyway, Zoe was quite capable of making her own decisions over who she went out with and seemed perfectly happy with her choice. In those days, we were still learning the gentle art of parenting and had only graduated as far as five and six year olds. We didn't feel qualified to be parents to a nineteen year old !

It was reassuring that Zoe was more than capable of looking after herself. She had told me several times that the experiences of the last few months had made her 'grow up'. The sense of indecision that had led her from one casual job to another, in bar work and disco dancing, had turned to determination and purpose when she had joined us. That had now transformed into greater wisdom and an ability to examine her options when she returned home.

Jorge had also told us that Ismael was the heir to a considerable family business and his parents were pillars of the local community. Any indiscretions would bring shame upon them which gave us as good a guarantee as we could get that he would behave himself.

This was fortunate because the close quarters canoodling they indulged in whenever they were together would have worried many parents.

As we reached the door to the roller skating rink a surprisingly crisp English voice boomed across the foyer.

"Well hello there !" We looked round, unsure that it could have been aimed at us but intrigued to identify anyone English, if only because we might glean a bit of news from home. One advantage of our recent misfortune was that we were never short of stories to share, even if we had nobody to share them with.

A tall, distinguished looking man was striding across the foyer towards us, his hand already outstretched. He wore a smart green hacking jacket of Harris tweed with leather patches over the elbows, tweed trousers, a neatly clipped grey beard and what could well have been an old school tie. He also carried in his wake two younger and more casually dressed men. They were shorter, stockier and with swarthy Mediterranean complexions.

He shook the three of us firmly by the hand before solemnly bending at the waist and politely shaking hands with Kim and Tania. I could swear Kim actually curtseyed before huddling shyly up to my legs with Tania, each holding on to one of my hands.

The stranger smiled benevolently down at them for a moment before returning his attention to adult level. He complimented us on their courteous behaviour before checking that we were the people he thought we were. George nodded, lifting the peak of his old blue cap; always an indication he was more than slightly intrigued by the turn that events were taking.

The man spoke confidently and with a clipped Home Counties accent. "I happened to be in the area and heard about your ... um ... misfortune." He smiled sympathetically, confirming that such misfortune brought with it some sort of opportunity. He paused, testing for an immediate response. We took our lead from George and said nothing. "I wondered if we might do a little business." Still, George said nothing, his interest signalled by nothing more tangible than a slight raising of one eyebrow. "Perhaps I should explain. I'm from Lloyds of London." He looked expectantly at each of us in turn. Still no reaction. The stranger was not to be discouraged. "Perhaps you would consider insuring your next boat – particularly as Salamander wasn't insured."

Clearly he had done some sort of research. George, despite his reticence, was interested enough to share a few more minutes with him. The man suggested we go somewhere more private to discuss 'things' in more detail. George drifted away from us with the three newcomers and I saw his expression turn to a smile. I overheard the tweed jacket man suggest they repair to the bar while Zoe and I took the girls for their skating session. George turned to me briefly and nodded reassuringly. He wouldn't be long, he promised.

I nodded. It isn't that George is a chauvinist. Far from it. It's just that we each know our own strengths. One of his was 'doing business' as he vaguely put it. I was quite happy to leave him to it, although I had already made up my mind what this epitome of all that is Oxbridge England was up to.

While Kim and Tania scorched round the skating rink, burning up surplus energy and slower skaters who were foolish enough to wobble along in front of them, Zoe and I compared opinions.

"It's just a joke isn't it ?" she suggested. "I mean, what are the odds ? A Lloyds insurance broker out here !" I wasn't so sure. "Come on Jean," she insisted. "What's he doing here ? He doesn't look like someone on holiday and as far as I know Lloyds doesn't have a branch in Porto !"

I could agree with her up to a point. "I don't think he's trying to sell insurance, that's for sure. But I do think he's got an angle. My bet is he's after Salamander for the salvage.

Maybe he's planning on giving us part exchange on another boat."

"Would you have another boat ?" It was a serious question and one that, until that moment, I hadn't considered.

I shrugged. "Never say 'never', I suppose. That's what George would say."

Zoe sighed and shook her head. "I reckon he's having a laugh. Some people have a really sick sense of humour. I bet John or Jorge has put him up to it."

I had to admit, that possibility had not crossed my mind, but it was too late to back down now. After all, Even though Zoe was a lovely girl and very sensible, she was only nineteen. She couldn't yet have the finely honed judgement of character I had. "Those two men with him," I went on. Zoe nodded. "Obviously, they're divers. If ever I've seen two men who make their living out of salvage, that's them."

Zoe laughed out loud. "Just because one of them is wearing a roll necked navy blue jumper, that doesn't make them divers !"

"It's not what they're wearing." I said, mustering as much dignity as I could. "I just know our luck is changing – and I know a diver when I see one." I sniffed and folded my arms. "You'll see. I've spent years around these people. Sailors, salvage men, divers; they all have the same... *air* about them." I seemed to have Zoe's attention and she had stopped contradicting. I decided to complete her education for her. "The smartly dressed one is the money man. He's going to put up loads of cash to buy the salvage rights to Salamander and the other two are his salvage team." I crossed my legs, turning slightly to watch the girls skeltering round the rink. I folded my arms and nodded decisively. I was glad I'd managed to clear that one up.

Zoe took the hint and said nothing. She wasn't going to burst my bubble.

At length George returned, shortly followed by the non-Lloyds man and the two divers. They all sat down a little distance from us holding a drink each, casually watching the skaters. The two divers chattered between themselves. I couldn't make out what they were saying or what language they were speaking.

Zoe and I slid along the bench and I nudged George. "Well ?"

He looked neither to left nor right. "The older chap with the beard," I nodded encouragement, nudging Zoe this time. George paused, sniffed and rubbed his nose, milking the moment. "He's in the music business." My shoulders fell. "The other one in the blue jumper; he's a road manager and sound man. The other chap is from Porto. He makes musical instruments and he's been trying to flog them to the bloke with the beard."

I looked at my feet. I felt Zoe's arm move gently round me as she gave me a hug. I let my head drop onto her shoulder and whispered in her ear. "Sorry."

She squeezed me a little tighter. "So am I," she whispered.

George shuffled slightly on the hard wooden bench. He reached inside his jacket as if to scratch his chest. I felt his arm move next to me and glanced in his direction. Peeping out of his jacket just below his broadly grinning face he held a large wad of bank notes. Gently replacing them, he nodded towards the roller rink.

"Get the girls my love. I'm taking us all out for a meal."

The music man, it turned out, was an impresario of open air festivals, for which – thank the Lord – he needed to provide a portable supply of electricity. Four days earlier his generator had interrupted a rehearsal with a loud clattering noise before exploding in a cloud of oily smoke. He only had another week to find a replacement or forfeit the money already raised from ticket sales. He and three rock bands, none of which any of us had heard of before, would all lose everything if he failed in his mission.

He had readily agreed to pay any necessary tax but seemed sure he would be able to avoid any payments in Portugal as he would be returning to the UK within a couple of months, taking the generator with him. His subterfuge at introducing himself as an insurance man had simply been a diversionary tactic. He had been warned of the problems we had been having with the authorities and was aware that several off-duty policemen would be at the Roller Hockey rink. The local police force fielded no fewer than three teams for local competitions and they often practiced here.

The instrument maker had offered to negotiate with the local authorities and complete any forms they needed. None had blinked at George's asking price of £500 nor at his tentative request for a deposit.

We added it to the £350 already paid towards the Opel car and trailer. When the remainder of the £500 was paid we would be close to paying the full £900 due.

Early the following morning, while George went off to give Saint Jorge the good news, Zoe and I began sorting once more through our possessions.

For the first time we knew with some certainty how much luggage space we would have. We could now make firm decisions over what we could take and what would have to be left behind. We marked out the size and shape of the trailer on the floor and carefully piled up those items we gave highest priority to. There were sleeping bags, our new tent, groundsheet (which would go over the top as protection from the weather) clothes, the radar (the most valuable item remaining, providing it could be repaired and sold in Guernsey) and, as Kim and Tania firmly reminded us, two buggies, two dolls and two large teddy bears. They weren't so bothered about packing their water damaged school books, but I assured them we would manage to find a corner for them.

Zoe and I sat on the sofa and looked at the heap in the middle of the floor. George's words from the old narrow bridge came back to me. "All our worldly goods." I muttered quietly.

We were suddenly very homesick. The life for most women in and around Espinho was so different from anything we were used to – or ever likely to become used to. The average housewife seemed to spend at least five hours a day cleaning her home. Fernander's kitchen always looked dazzlingly bright and polished. When I first saw her cooker I assumed that either it was brand new or that she simply never used it. I had been wrong on both counts. She just cleaned it every day until it gleamed.

For the remainder of their day, these models of domesticity washed clothes in the stream, scrubbing them with soap and slapping them against the smooth rocks. Those who could afford to have someone else do their washing for them sat in small groups outside their front doors, unless it was raining, passing their time with crochet work or knitting. The common factor between these two groups and our Channel Island housewives being that, whatever their activity, it was invariably accompanied by hours of good juicy gossip.

Two days later, by arrangement, George walked to the beach and met the music man. He had promised us he would not only find a way of getting the generator out of Salamander, but would foot any bill necessary to transport it wherever he needed to take it.

There, waiting next to Salamander's hull, stood the means of extraction that, for months, had alluded us. Our neighbour the farmer, his team of three oxen and a small army of willing workers (some of whom might have been there simply for the spectacle) were busying themselves with lengths of rope, a large block and tackle and a pyramid shaped frame of stout timber, already perched above the large hole cut in Salamander's hull.

The rope was threaded through this makeshift hoist, down into Salamander's engine room and made fast on the generator's iron mounting. George had already taken the bolts out which held it in place and it was a simple matter for the farmer to coax his beasts into movement and lift the entire assembly free.

Like a giant sinewy hand extracting a blockage from a sink, the generator, encased in rope and dripping oil and water, emerged from the bilges. While the oxen stood their ground, it was pulled on the end of a second rope by the concerted efforts of the assembled audience, away from the deck and lowered onto the back of a waiting truck. The entire operation took no more than forty minutes.

The music man seemed delighted, inspecting his new acquisition with the satisfied eye of one who has become used to improvising. He happily handed over the remaining purchase price to George who, having shaken the hand of everyone on the beach, hastened away in the direction of the Opel Rekord.

Zoe, the girls and I walked more slowly back to the village, discussing our final travel arrangements.

When George returned to the apartment, it was immediately clear that not all had gone according to plan. The Portuguese rate of inflation had been running amuck for years as had the international exchange rate. One Escudo was now worth less than a penny – and the cost of the precious Opel had consequently risen steeply. After George had finished scribbling figures on the back of an envelope, he announced gloomily that it had risen from the equivalent of £900 and would now cost £1,117. As we had been paid by the music man in sterling, we were over £200 short.

He slumped onto the sofa, deeply annoyed with himself. He should have done his sums earlier and adjusted the generator's asking price.

I sat down next to him, once more to make the latest reassessment of our financial situation. What emerged was yet more in a long series of lists. If nothing else, we were helping to keep the Espinho stationery shop afloat ! I had lost count of the number of times we had studied our road maps and calculated the number of gallons of petrol we would need. We now checked and double checked the price of fuel in Portugal, Spain and France. We confirmed, as far as we could from our back issues of Channel Island newspapers, the cost of ferry crossings to Guernsey. We made careful assessments of the number of nights we could stay in camp sites and the number of nights we would sleep in the car or by the roadside – or not stop at all. We added up the price of food from cafés and in tins plus the cost of camping gas.

Whichever way we did our sums, after scratching together all of our spare cash and having added the cost of buying the trailer, we were almost £300 short.

We looked again at our pile of possessions, still piled on the trailer shape on the floor. Toys, bedding, clothes and the radar might all have to stay behind. Financially speaking, that would be the greatest disappointment. The money we could get from selling everything once we got home would have given us a new start.

The girls looked up at us with those big eyes of theirs. Call me soft, but we knew there would always be room enough for a teddy bear or two.

We re-launched our sales campaign in a last ditch attempt to get the remaining funds together before either the price of the Opel went up again or we had to spend what little money we had on food.

Once more, we called upon Saint Jorge for help. The dilemma explained, we asked him to make one final effort to find anyone who might want to buy any of the remaining equipment, regardless of how small or cheap it might be. We would be prepared to accept virtually any price for anything we had, just so long as we could raise enough. Jorge sat for a moment, apparently lost in thought.

"I have an idea." He pointed to a scrap of paper with our latest list of figures. "I think I know this man with the Opel." We nodded. Jorge had been our translator and negotiator in chief throughout our transactions. "This is what I think we may do..."

He went on to describe a deal as simple as it was cheeky, and one that we would never have dared suggest. We should first make sure our calculations were correct and that we had enough ready cash for the trailer and the journey home. Under Jorge's plan, anything we had left over would be paid to the car owner. He would then act as guarantor for any outstanding amount due. He was sure he could get an agreement, especially if we promised to pay an extra £50 if all of the £217 due wasn't paid by 31st January.

Zoe looked at me and George. We both nodded dumbly and George stuck out his hand to shake Jorge's.

"Jorge," he said "you really are a bloody Saint."

I'm not so sure Jorge quite understood, but he blushed modestly anyway.

After Jorge left, George turned to me triumphantly. "There you are." He said. "I told you it'll be all right."

I nodded and clutched his arm. "You did, George. You did."

Chapter Six

On the Move Again

The Opel and trailer arrived a few days later and we gleefully began packing everything we could. Our transient life-style had enabled us to develop a certain degree of skill for such tasks. Admittedly the back axle was nearly touching the ground and there was barely enough room for an adult and two children to squeeze into the back seat. There was barely a cubic inch left unfilled, but we eventually found a space for everything that had been on our list.

We would leave, we decided, at 8 am on 12th January. Even that most simple part of the plan, fate decided, was too ambitious. Although we had spent most of the previous day making the rounds of Espinho saying our farewells (Zoe's goodbye to Ismael took the longest) come sunrise, most of the village turned out to see us on our way.

Gifts were exchanged. There were hugs, kisses and more than a few tears. By the time we were able to pull ourselves away several hours had passed.

Ismael, already established as a firm favourite with Kim and Tania as well as Zoe, bent down and whispered to Kim.

"Remember now," he said, "you come back to Espinho." We all nodded. Ismael winked. "And I arrange our wedding, yes?"

Kim gasped audibly, looking up at me for guidance. As usual, she found her own answers. She frowned earnestly.

"But," she said thoughtfully, "I'm too small."

"That is no problem." Ismael smiled. "My father has a shoe factory. He will have his top man to make a pair of boots with big big heels. We will make you tall."

Kim thought for a moment longer. "But I can't get married. I can't cook."

"That is no problem too! I cook and you do washing up. OK?" He smiled and ruffled her hair. Zoe kissed him on the cheek.

"There!" Kim announced triumphantly. "I can't marry Ismael. Zoe kissed him!"

This dilemma resolved, George made his final check of our luggage and circled the car once more. One large hand covered his face and he pointed in disgust towards the rear corner of the car. One of the tyres, perhaps unaccustomed to such a heavy load, was flat. Everything had to be unloaded from the boot to get to the spare wheel, the jack and the few tools we had saved from Salamander's toolkit.

Wheel replaced and boot re-loaded, we all piled back on board. George cheerfully said he hoped, now the spare tyre was punctured, that we wouldn't run over any nails on the way and turned the ignition key. The starter clicked a couple of times and fell silent.

Ismael squatted down so his head was next to the open window. "You know, George, the lights are on."

George punched the steering wheel. They had been on all night. The battery was flat. John came to the rescue with jump leads and, finally, having convinced ourselves the battery and all other essential parts were in good enough condition to re-charge it as we drove, we got the engine running.

It had been just over 21 weeks since we had left Guernsey and 18 of them had been spent in Espinho. As my eyes filled with tears, Saint Jorge put his head through the car window one last time and kissed me on the cheek. He must have tasted the salt water as he immediately looked up at George.

"I think George, you cannot go. Jean wishes to stay, no ?"

I gulped back my final rogue tear and almost shouted, "No !" With a final squeeze of our Saint's hand, I slapped the dashboard and commanded "Home, George. We're going home."

As we drove through the serene Portuguese countryside, heading for the Spanish border, we gained a far more appealing impression of the country than had been given by our home for the last four months.

We passed between magnificent high mountains that had been nothing but a dull blue-grey backdrop when seen from the coast. Fir trees and Eucalyptus lined the roads and seemingly tiny rivers weaved along, hundreds of feet below us. A flimsy fence was the only obstacle between us and a sheer rock face and certain end.

George didn't see much of the scenery. The cost of insurance for a second driver meant he had to do all the driving. I don't think he appreciated the comment I made (more than once) that the great advantage of travelling across land was that you got a far better view than from the sea.

Once again using the maps sent to us from Guernsey, I navigated without error (almost) across Portugal. George, of course, insists to this day that I took us by entirely the wrong route. My excuse is that we wanted to see as much of the country as possible, having been stuck in such a small area for so long.

We found the main highway to Vilar Formoso, around 120 kilometres east of Espinho, at around 7 pm. The border lay about the same distance ahead of us but, at my insistence, we stopped at the next lay-by for a rest. We had planned a route that got us out of Portugal as quickly as possible. Apart from wishing to reduce the chances of transgressing any more of their laws, Spain's petrol was also a lot cheaper.

By way of survival rations we had taken with us a jar of honey. Unlike the Owl and the Pussycat, however, we didn't have lots of money wrapped up in a five pound note. Instead, we had a tub of margarine, 20 bread rolls and a few tins of pears. They might not have been so poetic, but at least the children would enjoy them and the pear juice would quench their thirst.

After a rudimentary supper the girls were wrapped snugly into their sleeping bags – which, we discovered, take up a remarkable amount of room in the back of an Opel Rekord.

The girls slept like two small logs while the rest of us, being unable to stretch out, dozed on and off until around 7 am.

We awoke in bitter cold. Ice had formed inside the windows and we had to scrape small holes with crumpled up paper bags to peer out. A light sprinkling of snow covered the fields next to our lay-by. The road was covered in ice and, to my dismay, George announced that it hadn't occurred to him to check whether we had any anti-freeze in the radiator.

Pulling a blanket closely round him, he opened the door and negotiated the icy surface of the lay-by until he reached the front of the car. He lifted the bonnet and gingerly took off the radiator cap. Peering into the darkness, he poked a pencil into the hole. He decided the contents seemed reasonably liquid. Returning to his driving seat, he breathed heavily on his hands to warm them. "That," he warned us sagely "doesn't mean the water in the block hasn't frozen."

It hadn't occurred to us, in southern Europe, that we might encounter freezing weather. Neither, apparently, had it to any of our friends from Espinho who had spent several days advising us of the best route across country and potential hazards to be wary of. Clearly their suggestions had been based on avoiding pot-holes rather than icy mountains.

We debated whether we should wait for the sun to rise a bit further in the hope of a thaw, but concluded we could be waiting hours and still be none the wiser. There was no guarantee at this time of year and at this altitude (we estimated we were about 2,000 feet above sea level) that the temperature would rise above freezing point, even by early afternoon.

Gingerly, George turned the ignition key. By some miracle, the car started easily and first time. We eased away, keeping the revs down to avoid skidding and putting as little pressure on the engine as possible. Perhaps we should do yet another calculation of our funds and include the cost of a bottle of anti-freeze.

George watched with growing concern as the needle rose steadily up the temperature gauge. As it crept closer to the red line and I tapped at it, asking if it was working properly, George explained. There must be ice in the radiator, so there wasn't enough water actually circulating round the engine and keeping it cool. Ironically, in those freezing conditions, we had to free-wheel wherever possible for the first twenty miles or so to avoid over-heating. Even after the ice had fully melted, the temperature gauge continued to creep higher as the engine strained against the huge payload we unfairly expected it to pull and the slope in the road that took us ever higher.

Despite regular stops to cool down, we managed to make it over the highest peak and coasted downhill for the last few miles to the Spanish border. Not for the first time, I felt enormously proud of George's perseverance and sound judgement.

We passed through customs and immigration without incident. I could see George visibly relax as we drove away from the Spanish customs point. This had been Portugal's last opportunity to slap a tax bill on us or confiscate any of our possessions. We felt altogether more reassured in Spain. Since her Monarchy had been restored in 1975, the excesses of Franco's military regime had been all but expunged and the country now had a feeling of liberation about it.

George often spoke of his parents' experiences in occupied Guernsey during the last war and their indescribable relief at the liberation. I'm sure no Spaniard would have compared Franco to the German occupation, but their joy at liberalisation was unmistakeable.

For us, Spain meant a friendlier police force, cheaper petrol and a route to France, St.Malo and the ferry home.

The journey through the Spanish countryside passed with an unusual absence of incidents and we managed to find most of the main roads we had planned out on the map.

From time to time, while George allowed the engine to cool, Zoe and I switched places so she could navigate while I sat in the back with the girls. We passed through San Sebastian in northern Spain as the sun dropped on a pleasantly sunny and mild winter's day. We made the decision to press on for the French border.

We filled the tank with petrol, petrol prices being that bit higher in France, and before long had joined a long queue of lorries, caravans and other holiday makers waiting to pass through the formalities of immigration and customs.

For once, we had no worries over either. We were about to enter a Common Market Country; one of Britain's European partners, as Edward Heath had kept assuring us during that era when we had been persuaded that the Common Market was a good club to join.

We had nothing to declare to customs as everything on board was destined for Guernsey. We had spent so many holidays in France during the years before the girls were born, we felt sure we were now on even friendlier territory.

George stretched languidly in the driving seat. We had battled with men in uniform right round the coast of France, Spain and Portugal. A couple more wouldn't make any difference.

We reached the head of the queue and were quickly waved through the Spanish checkpoint. We waved politely to the officer as he gave us a half hearted salute and beckoned the next vehicle through.

Up ahead lay the French border and traffic seemed to be moving through fairly freely. At that time of the evening, in mid winter, there were relatively few officers on duty and the one or two we could see were already glancing at their watches and waiting for the next shift to take over.

The immigration officer glanced briefly at our passports, held aloft as we approached the barrier, and waved us through.

We joined the next part of the queue and, as we reached the front of the line, a Gendarme raised his hand. My heart missed a beat as he waved us to the side of the road and pulled a clip board from the window of the small portable shed that served as an office.

George wound down the window as the officer approached and touched the peak of his cap. He spoke in French, having identified our international registration plate and, presumably, being unable to speak Portuguese. He wished us a good evening and asked for our papers.

"Bollocks."

I heard George clearly from my position in the back seat, so I was quite certain the officer must have heard just as easily. George shuffled some papers from one pocket to another before handing over a thick wad of documents.

The officer thanked him and retreated a pace or two to inspect them under the street light.

"What did you give him ?"

"Everything. The temporary visas from Porto, all the tax papers, the log book for the car, the motor insurance, Salamander's salvage papers, the receipts from the orphanage. Everything."

It was hardly surprising the officer's face was becoming more and more creased with confusion. He looked at each of the documents in turn, flipping them over, then squinting closer, reading the fine print. Whether or not he could understand them, it was clear before long that, whatever papers he was looking at, they were not the ones he wished to see.

At length, the Gendarme's face re-appeared at George's window and he handed back the wedge of papers. "Pardon monsieur. Avez vous les papiers d'automobile ?" He pronounced his words slowly and crisply so there could be no confusion.

George nodded obligingly and returned a single sheet selected from the pile he had just had returned. It was the insurance document issued in Porto.

There was only one small technical detail likely to cause concern. Our insurance only covered George to drive in Portugal. We had been lucky in Spain, but it seemed that luck had just run out.

The officer shook his head patiently. "Non monsieur. Les papiers por La France s'il vouz plait."

George assumed his best 'confused foreigner' expression and shook his head. "Si, si. Esta par La Franca"

The officer's head shook again. A note of intolerance crept into his voice. "Non monsieur." He beckoned to another officer standing between two police cars. They had a brief discussion, glancing uncertainly around at us before he bent down once more. He told us we had to go with the other officer to a police station. The nearest one was at the next town, Hendaye.

"Que ? Por Favor ?" asked George, with an air of injured innocence.

The officer pointed abruptly at one of the police cars ahead of us. "Allez vouz en !" The officer made a final attempt to be civil. "Si'l vouz plait, monsieur. Merci." He beckoned us sharply to move forward and make way for the next car.

George shrugged. "D'accord."

He rolled the window up and exhaled deeply. I wondered why he had conceded so easily when clearly we were about to be held up for several hours and would probably get a fine as well. He seemed to anticipate my question.

"If I'd argued any more, the chances are I would have been arrested on the spot you lot would have been stranded here. This way, we may just get away with it."

I was tired and the prospect of a night in a police station didn't appeal. I folded my arms huffily. "I don't see how."

Patiently, George explained. The policemen had judged, quite correctly, that neither of them would be able to fit in the car with us. Three adults, two children, bedding from several nights spent on the road and various items of luggage had all made sure of that.

The Gendarme was waving us on again, pointing to the police car in front and directing us to follow. As we drove, George explained he had heard just enough of the discussion between the two officers to know they had been arguing over who should accompany us. Neither had wanted to travel back to town and face the prospect of several hours paper-work. Only one of them would be accompanying us.

Obediently, George followed the patrol car up a slip road and joined the main coastal highway. A mile or so further north, the police car started to indicate that it was turning off the dual carriageway towards Hendaye. George flicked the right hand indicator on, his foot easing off the accelerator.

As the patrol car crossed the dotted white lines and headed down the slip road, George dropped down into third.

"Hang on." He flicked the indicator back again and pushed his foot hard down. The old Opel responded well and we gathered speed, pulling into the middle lane and overtaking a line of slow moving lorries and vans. The distance between us, the border, Hendaye and the police car gradually increased.

We didn't slow down or dare look behind us for fifty miles. We whistled through Biarritz with the speed of those who know the prices in such fashionable French resorts and have no Francs in their pockets. We just had to hope the natives wouldn't know that we were escaping from the law.

We streaked through the flat French countryside even quicker than we had through Spain, reaching St.Malo in just over ten hours.

4

Chapter Seven

Welcome Home

We had eaten little since leaving Espinho, having to save all our money for petrol. The 20 small bread rolls we had taken with us had degenerated from being tasty snacks on the first day to bullet hard rocks by the second day. Even the margarine and honey had failed to soften them and we had eked out the remaining small change we had at roadside food stalls and transport cafés.

By the time we got to France we had salvaged just enough Francs for two paper cups of hot chocolate for Kim and Tania, bought from a vending machine at a rural train station.

It was with some relief, then, that we reached St.Malo and discovered we had enough Sterling for the ferry crossing to Guernsey with sufficient change to buy a couple of sandwiches and a cup of coffee on board.

Rolling off the ferry, we breathed a sigh of relief and, although Pope John Paul had not yet set the fashion, I wanted to jump out of the car, kneel on our home soil and kiss the tarmac.

However, it was now the turn of Guernsey's small brigade of uniformed officials to alter our plans.

The customs officers took one look at our trailer and pulled us out of the queue waiting to leave the docks. We explained where we had been and what was in the trailer. We told them of our exhausting drive (omitting the details of our 'misunderstanding' at the French border) and where we were going. (Only a few miles up the road, as it happens. So close yet so far...)

The customs officials retreated to their office with George to check various bits of paper and consider what had to be done. This time there was no escape. We had told them where we were heading. They had our passports. They had George.

After what seemed like hours, although George later told me it was only a few minutes, they all returned to the car.

George sat down heavily in the driver's seat and crossed his arms.

"They want 40 quid in duty."

"We haven't got that sort of money." I protested, as if that was reason enough to get exemption from paying.

"That's what I told them."

"I should think so too." I crossed my arms alongside George and together we stared straight ahead through the front windscreen. Strange scraping noises raised a question in my mind. "So what are they going to do ?"

George jerked his thumb over his shoulder. "They're already doing it."

I turned to look but Zoe answered my question. "They're taking the trailer off the back of the car."

George nodded to confirm Zoe's analysis. "They're impounding it until we can pay."

Now it was my turn for action. I jumped out of the car and marched to where the two officials were working on the tow bar.

"How can we pay you," I asked, "if you take the things we'll have to sell before we can get any money ?"

Neither officer looked up from their work. "Your husband has already asked us the same question, madam."

"Well, humour me. What was your answer ?"

The officer shrugged with no attempt at an apology. "How you pay the duty is your business madam, and no concern of ours."

I recognised the signs of frigidity brought about by the application of a uniform and decided to waste no more energy on further argument. Instead, I appealed to the humanity I assumed they must have, even if only during their off duty hours. I asked if I could get a change of underwear from the trailer for the girls. They had been wearing the same clothes for four days.

That was another error of judgement on my part. They had no humanity. Still without looking up, both officers simultaneously took a sharp intake of breath and shook their heads. They were so synchronised, perhaps the manoeuvre was part of their basic training.

"Do you have children ?" I asked.

"Whether either of us do or we don't, madam, makes no difference."

I returned to the car in a deep sulk and slumped into the passenger seat, arms folded once more.

"No good?" George asked, somewhat pointlessly.

"I'll say they're not. Give a man a uniform and he turns into a bloody bastard." I covered my mouth with my hands, looking in the mirror to see if the children had heard. Zoe's eyes were gazing back, wide with surprise. "Mummy didn't mean that girls. You mustn't use words like that." I turned to check they had understood. Both girls were curled up on the back seat with their heads in Zoe's lap. She gently stroked their hair, grinning at me.

Minus our precious trailer, we reached the home of our good friends, Helen and Brian Terriss later that day. They had been kind enough to offer us an indefinite and rent free stay with them while we found our feet again.

All we were able to offer them during the three months that followed of their unquestioning generosity were endless tales of our adventures and a gold fountain pen that George had been given by the Espinho Roller Hockey Team for his services as their masseur.

One of our first priorities was to recover the trailer from the marauding customs officers. This time, George feared, a bottle or two of Whisky would not oil the wheels of the bureaucratic machine. Instead, I called upon the good will of an old and dear friend, Bill Green.

Bill was a Guernsey Deputy – a sort of local Councillor, who I had known since we were 13. He listened to our story of woe with his customary sympathy and was more than happy to lend us £40. We soon settled our bill, recovered the trailer and sold the radar; one of our principal assets. The loan was duly repaid and we seemed well on our way to getting back to some sort of financial normality.

While George set about finding work, I wrote to anyone I could think of to ask if they knew where we might find accommodation. There was one small catch. We wouldn't be able to pay any rent until George got a job. As soon as that happened, I gave my word, all rent arrears would be paid in full.

On my long list of helpful contacts, Bill Green featured once again and he was one of the first to send a reply. As I read his letter, tears welled up and I found myself openly crying, for only the second time since leaving Guernsey.

He accused me of using our old friendship to try and 'jump the queue'. I didn't understand what he could mean and, as I read on, the confusion and hurt only grew. He said that he was not open to corruption and that it was an affront to his integrity that I should have asked him to 'pull strings'.

I read and re-read the letter a dozen times but still could make no sense of it. Perhaps he hadn't understood me. What queue ? What corruption ? What 'strings' was he talking about ?

It was several weeks later, when I was seeking some sort of explanation or solace for what was clearly a major, though unwitting, faux pas that a friend gave me the answers. She told me Bill was now the Chairman of the island's Public Housing Committee. He must have thought I was asking him to move us up the housing list. The idea was as ridiculous as it was dreadful. We hadn't even put our names down for public housing. Of all the injustices that had befallen us over the last few months, coming from one of my oldest friends, none had stung as much as this. I wondered how on Earth Bill could assume I would stoop so low. It was the last time I ever wrote to him.

We managed to sell the Portuguese Opel to a couple who wanted a left hand drive car for a tour round Europe and saved enough money to buy two push bikes, each with a child seat. They proved to be a far healthier and cheaper mode of transport than motoring, although not much fun in mid winter.

After three months with Helen and Brian, and with little progress being made towards finding other lodgings, we struck lucky once again.

Janet and Spencer Gelsthorpe were, respectively, a school teacher and a plumbing engineer. He could never quite accept the simple title of 'plumber' and with some reason. Both he and Janet were extremely well qualified and highly regarded in their fields.

With equal volumes of good timing and generosity, they announced that they were going to take an extended holiday to Canada and asked whether we would look after their home, including several horses and hens, in exchange for living in their house rent free. How could we possibly refuse ?

We were thus settled for a further three months, during which time I tended the chickens, collecting eggs each day and made sure foxes and local dogs were kept at bay. Meanwhile George managed to get kicked by one of the horses, trodden on by another and dragged round the paddock tangled up in a bridle by a third.

Apart from these minor equine disagreements we lived a settled and trouble free existence. Until, that is, Janet and Spence arrived home.

Neither of them were natives of Guernsey. As non-residents, they were permitted to live on the island only while they had forms of employment which the local authorities considered beneficial to the island's economy. In their case, Janet's work as a school teacher satisfied the requirements.

However, when they had left for Canada, she had had to tender her resignation, albeit on the understanding that she would be offered her old job back when they returned.

She had no sooner telephoned the school to tell them she was home, than they received a visit from the Department D'Etrangee (the branch of the Channel Islands police which deals with non residents). Spence was immediately arrested for being on the island illegally. The only reason that Janet was spared, apparently, was that a group of girls from Portsmouth on a hen-weekend in Guernsey had resulted in seven of them being arrested. As a result they had no spare accommodation for women prisoners and she was given bail.

The charges against her were later dropped when they confirmed she had applied again for her teaching job. Much to Spence's chagrin, plumbing engineers were not considered sufficiently valuable an asset to warrant a licence to live on Guernsey. The Police eventually set out the charges against him. We discovered they related to the period of three months when Janet had not been registered as a teacher – mainly because they were both in Canada.

As a 'foreigner', Spence was not given bail for fear he might slip the country. Taking a lesson from Saint Jorge's book of negotiation, George and I visited the both police inspector dealing with the case and the magistrate who had refused him bail. They both ignored all our explanations of how wholly unlikely the charges were and how ridiculous it was to believe he would skip bail. Spence had nowhere else to go and a growing diary of work his customers had patiently been waiting for him to undertake.

One after another we and our neighbours visited the police station and gave statements explaining why Janet had not been working during the three months in question. Over and over again, we put in writing that she and Spence had been in Canada. Janet produced their passports, showing the dates stamped when they entered and left Canada. Either the police didn't believe us, or they simply couldn't be bothered to do the paperwork. Yet to be paid her first salary, she could not afford a lawyer. We were all convinced, in any case, that the States legal system would soon exonerate him.

Spence was kept in the cells until a court date could be arranged when, the officer conducting the case confidently predicted, he would be heavily fined and deported to the British mainland.

On the appointed day, we all gathered in the small court room that accommodates the custodians of Guernsey's system of justice. Spence sat silently and alone in the dock. His normal healthy and robust frame seemed somehow to have shrunk and his broad shoulders sloped as he stared down at his feet.

Two days before, a lawyer had visited Spence in prison and informed him he had been appointed by the States to defend him. They had spent just half an hour in conversation and Spence had received no reassurance from him at all.

The magistrate entered the room. At the usher's command we all stood to attention. Everyone nodded and bowed politely to each other. The Clerk of the Court bowed to the Magistrate. The prosecuting and defending solicitors bowed first to the Magistrate and then to each other. The Clerk bowed to them and they to him. Nobody bowed to Spence.

The ritual finally complete, the Magistrate sat on his high leather backed chair and we were all permitted to sit. All, that is, except Spence.

The Clerk read out the indictment and asked the defendant whether he was guilty or not guilty.

Spence's voice seemed a little shaky, but he managed a loud and clear 'Not guilty'. A few bottoms shuffled uneasily on their seats and the magistrate let out a lengthy sigh of resignation. The Clerk asked in turn whether each of the lawyers was ready to proceed. They both confirmed they were. He turned to the Magistrate and repeated that both sides were ready to proceed if the court conceded to hear the case today. The magistrate looked wearily at his watch and asked whether there were many other cases listed for the same morning.

After some paper flicking and turning of pages in a desk diary, the clerk announced their timetable permitted sufficient time for the case to proceed.

"Very well." The Magistrate waved his hand lazily at the solicitors' bench, took off his spectacles and sat back in his chair.

The prosecution solicitor rose to his feet, clasped the lapel of his jacket with his left hand and read from his notes.

"If the Court pleases, this case concerns an offence under Section 235a of the Channel Islands (Non - Residents) Act of 1957." He cleared his throat. "Regulation 163 of the Habitual Occupations Regulations of 1964, sir, states quite unequivocally, that it is an offence for a non-resident..."

The case for the Crown droned on for a full 20 minutes before, finally, he announced that, may it please the Court, the case for the prosecution was complete.

It seemed not to please the court particularly, as the magistrate simply leaned forward, wrote a couple of lines on a notepad and looked up at Spence's solicitor. His voice dropped to a bored monotone.

"I suppose you have something to say on your client's behalf ?"

The defence produced a pile of witness statements that, together, looked more like a petition. They were signed by more than 40 people who stated they knew that both the defendant and Janet had been out of the country. They had seen them leave from the small island airport for Gatwick. They had received postcards and letters from them postmarked Niagara, Toronto, Montreal and Vancouver. They had telephoned them in Canada. They had seen their holiday snapshots and received gifts from them of Canadian souvenirs.

Spence handed his and Janet's passports to the magistrate for inspection. They bore the date stamp of the Canadian Immigration Department and that made by the British Immigration Service when they returned to Gatwick three months later.

He produced Greyhound bus tickets issued in Quebec and Montreal.

George was called as a witness. He had been waiting outside in the lobby, supposedly so he wouldn't hear what had already been said which would colour his evidence. He confirmed that the defendant, along with his wife Janet, had been absent from the islands for three months immediately following her resignation from work. He (George) and I, Guernsey residents and solid citizens, knew this as we had been staying in their house throughout that time.

The Magistrate held up his hand, halting the defence's case in its tracks. He scribbled another note, lowered his half framed spectacles and stared sternly over them at George.

"Mr Russell," said he, "I must warn you that you are under oath."

George met his gaze full on. He assured the Magistrate he was fully aware of that and repeated, word for word, what he had just said.

"I heard you the first time, Mr Russell."

"I was just making sure the court understood."

"I did understand you, Mr. Russell. I only hope you understand me. The penalties for committing perjury are serious."

To say George was taken aback would have been an under-statement. The Magistrate was our bank manager who had known George for over twenty years. We had spoken to him several times since our return to the island, especially over the last few months. He knew full well where we had been living and why.

Spence was found guilty, convicted on the strength of a uniformed police officer's statement that he had visited the house a few weeks earlier and, he insisted, had seen Janet there. His evidence was completely inaccurate. It may have been deliberate fabrication or, possibly, an honest mistake – although I for one never saw him nor any other police officer at the house. The only police to call had been three plain clothed officers who had come to arrest them a few days after they came home from Canada.

The experience served only to convince me that my little Guernsey had grown into a land of double dealing. No wonder Bill had thought I was trying to corrupt him!

After the court case, Janet was mysteriously refused her old job back, although it was clear there was a vacancy at the school and she had always been well thought of by the senior staff. Each job she applied for was politely but firmly rebuffed with little or no explanation from the State Education Board.

Spence and Janet were eventually spared the ignominy of deportation. Literally hours before their deadline was due to expire, Janet was offered a job teaching at a privately owned college. Despite being one of the best qualified secondary school teachers on the island, it seemed that the powers-that-be had decided someone whose husband was a convicted felon could not be trusted to educate their youngsters.

They didn't stay long on the island and Janet gave up teaching to pursue a more fulfilling career abroad. Guernsey deserved to lose two such able and hard working people and the island's loss was Africa's gain.

In the meantime, however, we decided we should give them some privacy. It was time to move on and, once again, friends came to the rescue.

Ron and Margaret Mauger (pronounced Major) offered us a holiday let. Although George had, by now, got a job as an engineer with a local bus company they refused to accept any rent.

We were on our way to recovery. We had repaid all the money we owed and decided it was time we repaid some of the debts of kindness we had been shown. We bought a yellow Morris Marina, gathered together our camping kit, including the tent bought in Espinho eight months earlier, and booked our ferry tickets.

We arrived in Espinho three days later and checked into the campsite that we had managed to avoid the previous December. It was now early August and the contrast in the weather could not have been more dramatic. No longer was it necessary to check where rivulets of rain were running or where puddles would gather. The sun bore down and we saw the village, quite literally, in an entirely new light.

We settled in a spot which, the last time we had seen it, had been under several inches of swamp. We quickly erected the tent, although we already felt we wouldn't need it. The sky was a rich blue, the air still and warm. We sat in the long grass munching sandwiches and Portuguese pastries. The following day we would wander into the village and renew old acquaintances.

That evening we settled into our sleeping bags, the girls cosily tucked in between us, content in the knowledge that, this time, we really were on holiday.

Next morning, the four of us awoke feeling strangely irritated. I looked across to George and my mouth fell open. George uttered one of his occasional oaths, as usual before I could cover the girls' ears, but which I hoped they would not understand.

Both our faces, and those of the girls, were blotched with red spots and swollen almost beyond recognition. The entire Espinho population of munching mosquitoes must have found their way into our tent during the night and were now the best fed insects in Europe. My hand went straight into my bag and pulled out a bottle of calamine lotion.

A hearty breakfast and several alternate splashes of cool water and lotion later, we dressed and made our way towards the village. No sooner had we started our stroll down the main street than the first voice shouted at us.

"El Capitano ! Jean, Kim y Tania !!"

The occupants of the little café at the end of the street came falling out onto the pavement and swarmed around us, pumping our hands, patting the girls on the head and leading us back to the café. A local mosquito remedy was produced and within hours the red rashes had subsided and we were once again being fed and watered in true Portuguese style.

It took fully two days to get from one end of the village to the other. We weren't permitted to pass a shop, café or bar without being beckoned in and plied with cakes and drink.

On the third evening, now fully recovered from the invading insects, we settled down for another night. We felt well fed and nicely relaxed with wine and port. Apart from our first morning, we hadn't had to prepare a meal for ourselves, having been made to feel more than welcome once again by Jorge, John, Fernander and even Aura who still showed no sign of remorse for pilfering our spaghetti. The children had been made much fuss of. Zoe's absence had been much lamented, especially by Ismael who had taken a day off work to meet us when he had heard we were back in town.

Salamander still lay stubbornly on the beach but, happily, there were no signs of any renewed onslaught from the officials of Porto. Her decks were now even barer than when we had left her. Rigging bolts that had once held the anchor chains to the decks had been removed and much of the wheelhouse had strangely vanished. Local children had adopted her as an impromptu adventure playground and swung on knotted ropes hanging down the side of her hull.

That evening we returned to the campsite, satisfied that Salamander was still providing the locals with a bit of amusement. We gave the tent a thorough spraying with an aerosol of insect repellent and settled down for the night, Kim and Tania curled warmly between us.

We were awakened in the early hours. A thundering, flapping, roar tore through the night. The tent shook violently, the walls first sucked inwards then, a moment later, out like a trumpet player's cheeks. The roof billowed up and out like a sail then crashed in towards us.

George pulled the door flap open slightly and narrowly missed being hit by a flying tent peg. He turned, shouting above the roar, to grab hold of the girls and get out. I didn't stop to ask why.

As we bundled out of the tent, Tania saw another of the tent pegs being pulled from the ground and grabbed the guide rope. At that instant, it and two of the other pegs lost their grip in the soft soil and the tent took off like the main sail on a square rigger. Held down by the two remaining pegs at the back, the tent, canvas, groundsheet, pegs, bedding and Tania all flapped then flipped upwards. They tore back then round, hurled about by the blasting gale. Tania's legs flailed in the wind and George grabbed out trying to get hold of her waist.

His hand closed on the waistband of her pyjama trousers and he hauled her towards him. Mercifully she let go of the rope and under his weight they fell back onto the grass. We all crawled into a relatively sheltered spot behind the car. Even that didn't seem all that safe as it bucked and rocked in the buffeting blasts of wind.

George crawled, Indian style, back to the groundsheet where the tent had once stood and scrabbled around for his keys. Back with us, he unlocked the car and we bundled inside.

As we sat huddled together it suddenly occurred to me that this wind actually seemed to hurt ! Every time a gust had hit me in the face it had felt like I had been stung, although no mosquito would be foolish enough to attempt to fly in these conditions, surely ?

We stayed sheltering in the car until sunrise when, as suddenly as it had started, the wind dropped. We let go of the girls' heads, which had been buried in towels, and risked a glimpse at what had, until that night, been our temporary home.

The tent was flattened against the six foot hedge that formed the boundary to the campsite. There were several tears running the length of the roof from the middle seam to the corners where the guide ropes had been attached. One of the aluminium poles was bent at right angles and our bedding was – Heaven only knew where.

We soon discovered that we had been introduced to The Mistral. This was the wind of legendary ferocity that blew clouds of hot Saharan sand across the Mediterranean into Europe. It had hit us, George said, like a tornado loaded with a jet of glass dust shot from a high pressure hose.

When we traipsed into the village later that morning we were greeted at Café Enfante by concerned questions from the owner and his family.

"Capitano... El Mistral... " was all he said. It didn't seem necessary to say any more. We just stood and shrugged at each other before sitting down to a particularly fortifying breakfast. With a certain sense of deja vu, we counted our losses.

That afternoon, we bowed to nature's awesome powers once more. We packed what remained of our camping gear and belongings, said our farewells and left.

A happy end was found, incidentally, for the tent. We gave it to one of Guernsey's troops of Girl Guides as a repair project. I was told some time later that many badges for sewing and camp-craft had been handed out as a result.

The following year, 1982, we once again made the trip south. George had been working for over a year by then and we were better financed and more organised. We had bought an ex-Army tent which, although not very attractive, was virtually bullet proof. We hoped we wouldn't have to test whether it was Mistral proof.

We travelled in a Scamp Jeep that George had converted so, if our heavy duty tent was blown away or otherwise damaged, four of us could sleep in relative comfort. We also took a variety of presents from Guernsey including, of course, a Guernsey; a thick and heavily oiled jumper guaranteed to keep out the worst of the Atlantic coast weather.

Of a more relaxed frame of mind now, on the way through France we stopped at an antique shop in a small village. Covered in dust at the back of a darkened back room was an old stone fireplace leaning against the wall. We stood inspecting it and, seizing his moment, the shop owner appeared and lovingly stroked his hand over the smooth stone.

It had, he told us, been taken from a 300 year old Breton farmhouse. It was believed that during the French Revolution escaping Parisian aristocrats had stopped at the house. The owner, professing to be a sympathiser had, for a fee, been prepared to take the risk of giving them shelter during their flight to England. It was just possible, the antique man nodded, that the Scarlet Pimpernel himself had warmed his feet before this very fireplace.

I looked at George. "I thought the Scarlet Pimpernel was just a character in a novel." He smiled and nodded. The shop keeper was quick off the mark. He raised his finger before we could spoil the picture further. "He is like your Robin Hood. He may not have been the very man Baroness Orczy wrote of, but there were many such heroes. English Aristocrats prepared to risk all to make fools of La Republique. As all outlaws were Robin Hoods – all these vagabonds were Scarlet Pimpernels. Oui ?"

We weren't sure whether to believe the story or not, but although the fireplace would have made a fine addition to our living room, we couldn't afford it. It remained unsold, gathering dust and provenance at the back of the shop.

Our holiday went well and, for once, was almost devoid of incident. On the return journey we stopped briefly for a meal in the small town of Ernee in northern France. There, in search of a parking space, we chanced on a narrow back street. Just behind the double doors of an old warehouse a middle aged man and his teenage son were hard at work –

making fireplaces exactly like the one the Scarlet Pimpernel had just possibly warmed his feet at. George and I watched for a few moments through the open doorway.

"Well," George said at length, "Sir Percy Blakeny must have found plenty of fires on his way between Paris and The Channel."

We asked whether the stonemason had based the design on an old Breton farmhouse style. The man smiled and put down his chisel.

"You have been talking to Etienne Duvois, non ?"

We shrugged and shook our heads in ignorance. He laughed a slow guttural laugh. "Mais oui. Duvois must have spoken to you. He tells all the tourists his fireplace is an antiquity. From the Revolution, oui ?"

We also smiled and nodded.

"Tell me," he closed one eye conspiratorially. "How much money did he ask ?"

We told him and, ten minutes later, walked out of the workshop with our very own Scarlet Pimpernel fireplace. We paid slightly less than a quarter of the original asking price.

Our fourth and final visit to Espinho took place in the summer of 1983. This time we travelled in an ancient converted furniture van.

But, perhaps, that's another story.

And Today

George and Jean have retired – from work, at least. They have, over the last 20 or so years since leaving Portugal, lived in Guernsey, France and Spain. They claim not to have found their Nirvana yet, but they keep looking.

They have now returned to their native Guernsey and are happily settled with their granddaughter and a small menagerie of pampered pets.

Zoe is still living in Guernsey. She is now married and has given up go-go dancing. Instead, she makes hand knitted Guernseys. It was one of hers that Jean took to Espinho in 1982.

Kim left home, having inherited her parents' wanderlust, at the age of 17. She lived for a while in a squat with a mixture of buskers, students and two tame rats. She currently lives in Yate near Bristol with her two younger daughters, Yanna and Tania.

Tania (senior) also lives in Guernsey and holds down three very different jobs. In the mornings she makes sandwiches in a small café and during the afternoons dresses Guernsey teddy bears for tourists. In the evenings she works as a carer at a Cheshire Home for the elderly.

For six weeks every year she goes to Africa where she works for Project Rhino. She has helped to establish conservation and development programmes across rural areas in Central and West Africa and to build a health clinic and water reservoir.

The Project was founded and is run by Jean and George's friends, Spence and Janet Gelsthorpe; the couple that Guernsey accused of not having a sufficiently worthy occupation between them to remain living there.

Jean and George report that they have come out of their experiences in Portugal as better and wiser people. More than ever before, they value the basic commodities of life.

Salamander is still a part of Espinho's scenery. She rests today where Jean and George left her in January 1981. As Yorkie had predicted, the tide has never climbed far enough up the beach to set her afloat.

She once again serves a useful purpose. Some might argue a more useful purpose than when she was mobile.

Today she supports a long slipway running from the top of the beach into the sea well below the low water mark. As it crosses the beach, the slipway's timbers have been built into and are supported by Salamander's hull.

Local fishermen and leisure sailors can now haul their boats directly out of the water or launch them, whatever the tide.

As they stroll past this local landmark, there are still those who remember the English family who brought Salamanda to their beach. They recall the two little girls, happily playing in the sand with local children and their pretty friend Zoe. And they remember the long nights of deep discussion and the quiet resolve of their parents, Jean and El Capitano.

And from time to time a tall, dark, well dressed and decidedly good looking middle aged man wanders down to the sea shore. He kicks his hand-made patent leather shoes over the pebbles, gazes up at Salamander's broad hull and rubs absently at a twinge in his right knee; the result of a violent goal-mouth clash during a long forgotten Roller Hockey match.

He wipes the occasional tear from his eye, kidding himself a grain of sand is the cause, and holds his teenage daughter's hand that little bit tighter.

In answer to her often repeated question, he promises her, one day, he'll explain why he named her Zoe.

Printed in the United Kingdom
by Lightning Source UK Ltd.
113674UKS00002B/1-72